breakingthemold

EMBRACE YOUR UNIQUE IDENTITY & EMPOWER YOUR MINISTRY

For DArLene
God's Best AlwAys

Bill McRay

BILL McRAY

breakingthemold

EMBRACE YOUR UNIQUE IDENTITY & EMPOWER YOUR MINISTRY

BILL MCRAY

breakingthemold
EMBRACE YOUR UNIQUE IDENTITY & EMPOWER YOUR MINISTRY

First Printing 2009

A Bill McRay Publishing Publication

Unless otherwise indicated, all quotations in this volume are from the King James Version of the Bible.

ISBN: 978-0-692-00271-1

Table of Contents

Acknowledgements

Grateful acknowledgement is given to my wife and co-pastor, Linda, who has traveled this journey with me for almost half a century. You are the love of my life and the greatest partner any man could ever have.

Huge thanks to the congregation of Victory Fellowship Church of Nashville, Tennessee. You have followed the leadership of this ministry for over thirty years, and most of what I know experientially about the local church I have learned from you. Your faithfulness has brought forth much fruit in the lives of many people. May you continue to grow and prosper in Him as we continue our journey together.

To Reverend Maryann Moore, my gifted editor, my deepest appreciation. You have served me so well for so many years on so many projects, and so unselfishly. Thank you for making my ramblings make sense. You are the best. To Jean Birdsong, our gifted proofreader, thank you for making me look smarter and more literate than I am. Thank you also for being a faithful sheep for so many years. To Vickilynn Gillette, our church secretary, thank you for all that you do to make your pastor look like he knows what he is doing. My gratitude goes to Kelley Mathis for reading and re-reading this manuscript. Your insights and suggestions have been helpful and much appreciated. To Beth DeLemos, thank you for stepping into this project at it's end to take care of the many last minute details. Last, but far from least, I want to thank my close and cherished friend, Pat Butcher, for agreeing to write the foreword for this book. Pat, you have no idea the blessing you are to so many. As a fellow apostolic pastor, I know your heart and your works, and they are both good.

Foreword

Pastors Bill and Linda McRay have been my friends for 25 years. In that time they have become more than friends, they are now my mentors. As a young Pastor, I had many questions and the feeling of inadequacy. Always, without hesitation, God used this seasoned couple to help! I remember one time when I had a couple in this new church that was out of sorts. For days, weeks and months I had been trying to find a sensible, Godly solution. I asked Pastors Bill and Linda to come up. They drove three and one half hours, met with the couple for 15 minutes, and by the grace of God, settled the issue. Wow! Wisdom, understanding and experience all in one place! It was then that I began to really watch and study their lives. Their heartfelt desire to see each Christian find their place in God's kingdom, especially Pastors, astounded me.

As the Lord Jesus began to reveal truths to Pastor Bill, I saw an evolution start to form. Sayings such as "being comfortable in your own skin" and "it's okay if you don't like hospital visitation" really opened my eyes. Why? Because on the inside I was miserable. Although I had a somewhat successful church in a small Kentucky town, I was uncomfortable and afraid to admit it. Pastor Bill kept encouraging me to be honest and face my strengths. You see, I have in my heart to plant churches, even before it was the "thing to do." I felt like a draft horse, weighing a ton, stuck in the starting gate at the Kentucky Derby. The key word was I was stuck.

Life and ministry are short. Constantly feeling stuck or not fitting the mold is frustrating. *Breaking the Mold* does exactly as it says. The revelation of the different giftings of Pastors began to give me the courage I needed to be me! Slowly I came out of the mold of a traditional, small town Pastor and faced my strengths, one being that I am called to plant churches. Wow, what a relief to finally come clean.

Every Christian needs to see their Pastor from God's point of view on how He created them. Once we as the body look to the gifts, talents and abilities of those who lead us, and not just to the traditional title, we begin to see the freedom to flourish and be who God called us to be. Go with your strengths, label your weaknesses and begin to lead with joy, freedom and truth. Be "comfortable in your own skin."

Sounds like our future is bright! Let's all begin to break the mold so the Master can release us to His harvest.

— Pat Butcher
Senior Pastor
Family Worship Center, Carrollton, KY

Introduction

It is my desire that the thoughts and insights reflected on the pages of this book will help the Body of Christ to come into a richer understanding of who we are in Christ Jesus, what we have in Him and what we can accomplish in and through Him. None of us are the same. We are each a unique creation of God. We are gifts that have gifts according to His purposes. With the revelation that is pouring into the earth in these days, the term "Body of Christ" is taking on a far greater significance, both in the Church and in the world.

In Ephesians 5:27 the Apostle Paul says that Jesus is returning for *a glorious church, not having spot or wrinkle,* that is *holy and without blemish.* This scripture implies that there are many changes that must occur in the Church. I yearn for those changes. My heart cries out for them. I am sure that yours does as well. I believe that we have entered into the "Last Days." I believe that it is not only a possibility, but a very high likelihood that Jesus could come in our lifetime. If that should be true then the Bible has much to say about this generation of believers. In I Corinthians 12:18 we are told that God has set every member in the Body with a purpose for His plan.

1 Corinthians 12:18

But now hath God set the members every one of them in the body, as it hath pleased him.

Each of us is what we are and who we are by God's pleasure. He set every person in the Body of Christ with gifts and He does not want the gifts that we are and the gifts that we carry to be hidden from us. It is beyond the time for us to know and acknowledge where we fit into the Body of Christ. We must become aware of the giftings that we carry and how each gift is supposed to function.

I struggled for years attempting to discover and understand my gift. As a pastor, people tried to mold me into an image of their perception of the gift of a pastor. Not knowing any differently, I also tried to mold myself into what I perceived a pastor to be. Both the people and I were unsuccessful in our efforts. I did not fit either mold. That created frustration for all of us. We all had our preconceived ideas of what a pastor should look like, how he was supposed to act and how he should conduct his ministry.

I was absolutely sure that God had called my wife, Linda, and me to plant and pioneer a local church in Nashville, Tennessee. Those were His clear instructions to us in the spring of 1977, just prior to my graduation from Bible college. In obedience we returned to Nashville, and the local church that we have now pastored for thirty-two years began on the second Sunday of June in 1977.

When God gave us the instructions to start a local church, He did not give us a diagram on how to do it. I knew that I was called to pastor, but I did not seem to fit the role of a pastor. I loved to preach and teach. I also loved to minister to people corporately and one-on-one. I lived to do those things. I did not even mind the administration and business side of pastoring a local church since I had been a business executive for years before entering the ministry. However, I did not fit in the realm of the other responsibilities that we believed a pastor was required to do, particularly regarding pastoral care responsibilities. I knew that the sheep must be tended to in those realms. I learned that I was gifted to feed and lead the sheep, but I had no anointing to tend them, or to take care of their personal and family needs. Many of my parishioners questioned how I could be a pastor and yet not be anointed to tend to my sheep in these areas.

Through the years I have learned that I am not the only pastor to ever come up against this frustration. I discovered that many other pastors were, and are now, struggling with the same issue. I am happy to say that the Lord was gracious and merciful in bringing light to the struggle in my soul. I pray that this message will also help those that have experienced the same quandary.

Over a period of years I taught on the five-fold ministry gifts and the pastor/sheep relationship in various ministers' conferences and Bible schools. As I did, God began to give me supernatural insight into the amazing diversity of His ministry gifts. In *Breaking the Mold* I share these insights with you. My desire in writing this book is to show you how to "break the mold" of preconceived ideas and misunderstandings that have held so many pastors and their congregations in bondage to unrealistic expectations. I believe that you will find these insights to be extremely simple, and yet deeply profound. I did!

Let me add that this book is not just for pastors. The principles revealed here are true for all ministry gifts and that includes the whole body of Christ. All believers are gifts, having gifts. I intend to encourage every current member and every new member of my church to read this book in order to better understand how to relate to me as their pastor and to the leadership of their church. As for me and my house, we are breaking the mold and building the Church!

CHAPTER ONE

Jesus, the Fullness of God

Many pastors that I know have suffered through and struggled with preconceived ideas of how the ministerial gifts are supposed to function. Many anointed and gifted ministers find that they do not fit the mold that has been framed for them through generations of tradition. As a result they struggle with such thoughts as, "There must be something wrong with me! I must not be called to be a pastor because I do not act or think like I have been taught that I should!"

One of the greatest struggles that any minister has is an understanding of who he is and what he is called to do. In order to understand who we are, we must first come to the understanding and revelation of *Who* and *What* Jesus is. Just as there is a *Who* and a *What* involved in the identity of Jesus, there is also a *who* and *what* involved in our identities. We must understand both to successfully operate in our gifts.

The New Testament revelation of Jesus Christ forms the foundation for the revelation of who we are in Him. Believers are not just men, women, boys and girls. We are new creations in Christ with the ability to produce much fruit. Without Him we are mere human beings, and according to the scriptures in John 15:4, 5, we can do nothing of eternal value.

John 15:4-5

Abide in me, and I in you. As the branch cannot bear fruit of itself, except it abide in the vine; no more can ye, except ye abide in me.

I am the vine, ye are the branches: He that abideth in me, and I in him, the same bringeth forth much fruit; for without me ye can do nothing.

For those of us who are in Christ Jesus, we have been given the great promise of our redemption as recorded in the second book of Corinthians.

2 Corinthians 5:17

Therefore if any man be in Christ, he is a new creature: old things are passed away; behold, all things are become new.

There are three truths that must become realities to us if we are to attain the abundant life that Jesus came to provide for us and to fulfill the plan of God for our lives. Those truths are who we are in Christ, what we have in Christ, and what we can do in Christ. The New Testament is filled with that revelation, but for it to become reality to us we must first have a revelation of Who and What Jesus is. The Apostle Paul gives a vivid picture of the make-up of Jesus Christ in Colossians 1:9-19 and 2:9, 10.

Colossians 1:9-19

For this cause we also, since the day we heard it, do not cease to pray for you, and to desire that ye might be filled with the knowledge of his will in all wisdom and spiritual understanding;

That ye might walk worthy of the Lord unto all pleasing, being fruitful in every good work, and increasing in the knowledge of God;

Strengthened with all might, according to his glorious power, unto all patience and longsuffering with joyfulness;

Giving thanks unto the Father, which has made us meet to be partakers of the inheritance of the saints in light:

Who hath delivered us from the power of darkness, and hath translated us into the kingdom of his dear Son:

In whom we have redemption through his blood, even the forgiveness of sins:

Who is the image of the invisible God, the firstborn of every creature:

For by him were all things created, that are in heaven, and that are in earth, visible and invisible, whether they be thrones, or dominions, or principalities, or powers: all things were created by him, and for him:

And he is before all things, and by him all things consist.

And he is the head of the body, the church: who is the beginning, the firstborn from the dead; that in all things he might have the preeminence.

For it pleased the Father that in him should all fulness dwell.

Colossians 2:9, 10

For in him dwelleth all the fulness of the Godhead bodily,

And ye are complete in him, which is the head of all principality and power.

Jesus is the fullness of the Godhead bodily. In Him (God in human flesh) dwells the fullness of *Who* and *What* God is. That is why Jesus could say to his disciple, Phillip, in John 14:9, *he that hath seen me hath seen the Father.* No other human being can say that. Only Jesus can!

The Apostle John gives us his revelation of Jesus Christ in the first chapter of the Gospel of John.

John 1:1, 2, 14

In the beginning was the Word, and the Word was with God, and the Word was God.

The same was in the beginning with God.

And the Word was made flesh, and dwelt among us, (and we beheld his glory, the glory as of the only begotten of the Father,) full of grace and truth.

These scriptures declare that Jesus is the fullness of the Godhead bodily. The question is how did the fullness come to Him? We find those answers in the writings of both Luke and John.

Luke 3:21-22

Now when all the people were baptized, it came to pass, that Jesus also being baptized, and praying, the heaven was opened,

And the Holy Ghost descended in a bodily shape like a dove upon him, and a voice came from heaven, which said, Thou art my beloved Son; in thee I am well pleased.

John 3:34, 35

For he whom God hath sent speaketh the words of God; for God giveth not the Spirit by measure unto him.

The Father loveth the Son, and hath given all things into his hand.

When Jesus was water-baptized in the Jordan River by John the Baptist, He was also baptized in the Holy Spirit. The above scriptures make it clear that He received the Spirit *without measure*, full of grace and truth. From the fullness that He received, we are told that we have each been given a measure of His grace.

John 1:16, 17

And of his fulness have all we received, and grace for grace.

For the law was given by Moses, but grace and truth came by Jesus Christ.

I emphasize again that Jesus is the *fullness* of the Godhead in human form, having the Holy Spirit *without* measure, full of grace and truth. These scriptures state that out of His fullness we have received grace for grace, but just what does that mean? The phrase "grace for grace" may be a little blind to us. To find the answer to the meaning of grace we must explore the definition of biblical grace.

Grace According to the Measure

We begin by understanding that the natural man is a law-minded creature. The entire concept of grace is over our head. It takes a measure of grace for us to just be able to receive grace. Ephesians 4:7 gives us a step in making this more clear.

Ephesians 4:7

But unto every one of us is given grace according to the measure of the gift of Christ.

We can break this down into steps. First, Jesus is the fullness of the Godhead bodily. All that God *is* dwells in Him, that defines the gift of Christ. He is God in all His fullness in the flesh. Secondly, we as believers are told that from Jesus' fullness we have each received a *measure* or a *portion* of the *fullness of God*. We have also been given *grace* according to the *measure* of *the gift of Christ*. As a believer, we are a gift of Christ to His Body, the Church, and also a gift of Christ to the world. As a member of the Body of Christ we are unique. Each person is special and is graced for the unique gift of Christ that he is.

Paul goes into more detail in describing the gifts that have been imparted to the Body of Christ in 1 Corinthians 12:12-28.

1 Corinthians 12:12-28

For as the body is one, and hath many members, and all the members of that one body, being many, are one body: so also is Christ.

For by one Spirit are we all baptized into one body, whether we be Jews or Gentiles, whether we be bond or free; and have been all made to drink into one Spirit.

For the body is not one member, but many.

If the foot shall say, Because I am not the hand, I am not of the body; is it therefore not of the body?

And if the ear shall say, Because I am not the eye, I am not of the body; is it therefore not of the body?

If the whole body were an eye, where were the hearing? If the whole were hearing, where were the smelling?

But now hath God set the members every one of them in the body, as it hath pleased him.

And if they were all one member, where were the body?

But now are they many members, yet but one body.

And the eye cannot say unto the hand, I have no need of thee: nor again the head to the feet, I have no need of you.

Nay, much more those members of the body, which seem to be more feeble, are necessary:

And those members of the body, which we think to be less honourable, upon these we bestow more abundant honour, and our uncomely parts have more abundant comeliness.

For our comely parts have no need: but God hath tempered the body together, having given more abundant honor to that part which lacked:

That there should be no schism in the body; but that the members should have the same care one for another.

And whether one member suffer, all the members suffer with it; or one member be honoured, all the members rejoice with it.

Now ye are the body of Christ, and members in particular.

And God hath set some in the church, first apostles, secondarily prophets, thirdly teachers, after that miracles, then gifts of healings, helps, governments, diversities of tongues.

These scriptures, along with the scriptures in Ephesians 4:11, teach us that all believers are gifts having gifts. We do not get to choose the gifts we are or the gifts that we have. Only God decides. In 1 Corinthians 12:18 God emphasizes that by saying, But now hath God set the members every one of them in the body, as it hath pleased him. The measure of the gift of Christ is designated by God. The gifts described in these scriptures are ministry gifts that are headed up by the five-fold ministry gifts. Some of these gifts are found in 1 Corinthians 12:28, and all are mentioned in Ephesians 4:11.

Ephesians 4:11

And he gave some, apostles; and some, prophets; and some, evangelists; and some, pastors and teachers.

The individual gifts or the manifestations of the Spirit that we have received are identified in 1 Corinthians 12:4-11.

1 Corinthians 12:4-11

Now there are diversities of gifts, but the same Spirit.

And there are differences of administrations, but the same Lord.

And there are diversities of operations, but it is the same God which worketh all in all.

But the manifestation of the Spirit is given to every man to profit withal.

For to one is given by the Spirit the word of wisdom; to another the word of knowledge by the same Spirit;

To another faith by the same Spirit; to another the gifts of healing by the same Spirit;

To another the working of miracles; to another prophecy; to another discerning of spirits; to another divers kinds of tongues; to another the interpretation of tongues:

But all these worketh that one and the selfsame Spirit, dividing to every man severally as he will.

Jesus has set every believer into the Church of Christ as it has pleased Him. We have each been given grace according to the measure of the gift of Christ that we are. That grace is the manifestation or the gifts of the Holy Spirit with the enablements and anointings necessary to function in the measure of those gifts. All ministry gifts and all gifts of the Spirit reside in Him, as well as the anointings. All abilities and enablements also reside in Jesus. That is why He could say, "If you have seen me, you have seen the Father." (John 14:9) He also said, "Without me you can do nothing." (John 16:5) Jesus is the only one who can make those two statements because He is the fullness of God. However, in John 1:16 we are told, *"And of his fulness have all we received grace for grace."*

It is out of His fullness that every member of the Body of Christ has received a measure. Because of this great truth it becomes imperative for every believer to discover and begin to function in the measure, or the gift of Christ that he is. Ephesians 5:27

tells us that Jesus is returning for *a glorious church, not having spot, or wrinkle, or any such thing; but that it should be holy and without blemish.* I believe that is the Church that Jesus is coming for, not what has been seen by every generation of believers for two thousand years. No individual believer has ever been able to say, "If you have seen me, you have seen Jesus." But I believe that as the time of His coming approaches we will be able to say, "If you have seen the Church, you have seen Jesus."

Build On Your Gift

The Apostle Paul was aware of the measure of Christ that he was and depended entirely on the grace that had been given to him to accomplish his assignment in that gift.

I Corinthians 2:1-5

And I, brethren, when I came to you, came not with excellency of speech or of wisdom, declaring unto you the testimony of God.

For I determined not to know any thing among you, save Jesus Christ, and him crucified.

And I was with you in weakness, and in fear, and in much trembling.

And my speech and my preaching was not with enticing words of man's wisdom, but in demonstration of the Spirit and of power.

That your faith should not stand in the wisdom of men, but in the power of God.

Paul was a brilliant man. He was among the most educated men of his day. His resumé was beyond impressive, yet he counted all of that as nothing compared to the wisdom of God. Instead, he depended entirely on the grace that had been given to him according to the gift that he was. He was a "foundation layer," and he built his ministry upon this gift.

Regardless of whether you are called to the Body of Christ as a five-fold ministry gift or as a lay-person, you are a measure of the gift of Christ with a vital ministry. That is why the message of this book is important. You have been set into the Body of Christ as it has pleased Him, and the fulfillment of your ministry is *necessary* to the completion of the Body. How you accomplish the goals of your ministry is also important.

2 Corinthians 4:7

But we have this treasure in earthen vessels, that the excellency of the power may be of God, and not of us.

We know that without Him we can do nothing, but we must also remember that He has created us in His image and after His likeness. God has given us intelligence, talent, ability and the desire to be fruitful. Above all that, He has added grace according to the measure of the gift of Himself that we are.

The treasure that we have in our earthen vessels is the enabling power of the Holy Spirit with His giftings and not our natural abilities. If we allow these earthen vessels to rule, we will lean toward our own ambitions, intelligence, talents and abilities. If we yield to the Holy Spirit and His plan and purpose for our lives, we will draw on the grace that enables the gift of Christ that we are. Then He is glorified when we bear much fruit. The excellency of the power is of God and not of us.

The Pastoral Example

I am a pastor, so to illustrate what I say here, I use the example of the pastoral ministry. During the great teaching revival of the 1970's, 80's and 90's, a large number of churches from many different camps and organizations were pioneered in the United States and around the world. The pioneering pastors of those churches had different spiritual circles of influence, but most of them had something in common. Almost every one of them wanted to pastor a large church. I do not remember ever hearing a single one of those pastors say, "I hope God only gives me a small church!" Some have been quick to say, "Well, numbers are not important. It is not about numbers!" That may be true in a sense. The quality of a church is not measured in numbers. But influence is. Numbers represent people and the more people a church has, the greater is the church's influence. Most pastors that I know want their churches to have as much influence as possible. They want to reach as many people as they can; therefore they want their churches to grow. I believe that we all want to feel that our ministries are significant.

Over the last few decades, we have witnessed the rise of the mega-church and the influence that it produces. A mega-church is one that has two-thousand or more people in actual attendance at their week-end services. The vast majority of local churches are considerably smaller. Most of us would like for our churches to grow to that size. Because of that desire, an entire industry has grown in the church world that develops church growth conferences. In many ways this is a good and beneficial ministry. I have attended church growth conferences all over the United States in many different camps. I have learned some great principles in some and have been able to use those principles in my church. Those principles have been helpful and I am truly grateful for them. However, there is a major difference between learning and employing good church growth principles, and the attempt to try to clone a mega-church model and its pastor. That is the mistake I have seen too many pastors make.

There is one well-known mega-church pastor that has had great influence in the United States. I have personally attended two or three of his conferences. In those meetings I learned some great things and have been able to use them profitably. In each meeting that I attended, I clearly heard this pastor admonish those in attendance, "Do not go home and try to transition your church into mine. Learn what we are attempting to teach you and use what works for you in your church, but do not try to be us." It would be far more beneficial if people would hear and obey, but many do not. Instead of receiving the principles, they often come away from these meetings with a model and style that they take back to their churches. They attempt to become just like that pastor, and try to make their churches just like his. Beloved, that never works and the reason is because they do not have that pastor's gift.

I have visited a significant number of mega-churches in both conferences and in services. The one thing that they have in common is that each one is different! Even if these churches are from the same camp they are different. The reason is that each pastor has built his church on his own gift and not another person's gift. There is not just one model that works for all churches. There is not just one style that works across the board. You must learn to be yourself. Do not try to be someone else. We all follow someone, but following another person's ministry and example does not require us to try to be just like they are.

I had a spiritual father whose blessing to me goes beyond expression. I followed his example and ministry for half of my life, but I never tried to be like him. God has given me grace according to the measure of the gift of Christ that I am, and I am building my church on that gift—my gift. I strongly encourage you to do the same in whatever field of ministry your gift falls.

CHAPTER TWO

Five-Fold Ministry
& Traditions of Men

The Lord Jesus Christ is the head of the Church. He reigns from His position seated at the right hand of the Father. However, we are told in Ephesians 4:11, 12 that in the earth the Church is headed up by the five-fold ministry.

Ephesians 4:11, 12

And he gave some, apostles; and some, prophets; and some, evangelists; and some, pastors and teachers;

For the perfecting of the saints, for the work of the ministry, for the edifying of the body of Christ:

Each of these gifts is a measure of the gift of Christ. Each one is accompanied by powerful anointings and manifestations (gifts) of the Holy Spirit. I believe that the Apostle Paul lists these gifts in the order and progression in which the Lord Jesus set them in the New Testament Church.

In the beginning there were the Apostles of the Lamb, also called "The Eleven." Other apostles were added to those as each was called into ministry. Following the apostles were the prophets, then the evangelists, pastors and teachers in that order. I believe the order and progression was determined by the nature, character and mission of each of these gifts. As each gift began to function in its unique anointing and mission, it prepared and made the way for the next gift. Had the leaders of the Church continued in the New Testament plan of the Lord, we would have a very different Church today. Unfortunately, over the years the traditions of men have gotten in the way, disregarding the Word of God and fulfilling the prophecy of Jesus as spoken in Mark 7:13, *Making the word of God of none effect through your tradition, which ye have delivered: and many such like things do ye.*

The five-fold ministry gifts of the apostle, prophet, evangelist, pastor and teacher are not job descriptions. Each one is a powerful ministry gift essential to the perfecting, or maturing, of believers for the work of the ministry and for the edifying, or building up, of the Body of Christ. Unless these ministry gifts are scripturally recognized for what they really are and allowed to function in the power God intended, the Church can never become what the Apostle Paul proclaims in Ephesians 4:13-16.

Ephesians 4:13-16

Till we all come in the unity of the faith, and of the knowledge of the Son of God, unto a perfect man, unto the measure of the stature of the fulness of Christ:

That we henceforth be no more children, tossed to and fro, and carried about with every wind of doctrine, by the sleight of men, and cunning craftiness, whereby they lie in wait to deceive.

But speaking the truth in love may grow up into him in all things, which is the head, even Christ:

From whom the whole body fitly joined together and compacted by that which every joint supplieth, according to the effectual working in the measure of every part, maketh increase of the body unto the edifying of itself in love.

In Matthew 16:18, Jesus said, ...I will build my church; and the gates of hell shall not prevail against it. The primary way He has chosen to build His church is two-fold: through the local church and through ministry gifts. We see the birth of both on the day of Pentecost in Acts 2. A local church was immediately formed through a body of Spirit-filled believers and ministry gifts began to function through the ministry gift of the apostles. God's plan has not changed since that great day. The local church is still the building block of the Church, and the ministry gifts are still the mortar that binds it together.

The five-fold ministry gifts are charged with the responsibility to develop and perfect all the other ministry gifts in the body of Christ. The reason the great majority of the Church is still in the babyhood stage of spirituality with no clue as to what the measure of the gift of Christ that they are is because of the failure of the five-fold ministry gifts to function in the power of their offices. Most of the Church does not even recognize the office of the apostle and prophet as valid for today. The other three gifts are reduced to natural function for the most part, especially the office of the pastor.

Instead of pastors being set into the churches by the Lord as it pleases Him, equipped supernaturally with the anointing and gifts necessary to fulfill his responsibilities, most are turned into hirelings by church congregations or their committees.

The traditions of men have made the Word of God of no effect. Even many full-gospel believers, who doctrinally believe that the five-fold gifts are valid for today, in actual practice only recognize the evangelist, pastor and teacher. We give lip service to the apostle and prophet, but if someone claims one of these offices, you can just watch and see what happens.

Even the best Bible schools that teach the validity of all five gifts only offer specialized courses for the evangelist, pastor and teacher. This must change before the Church can mature into a church *without spot or wrinkle or any such thing* that the Apostle Paul spoke of. I believe that Jesus will not return for anything less.

The five-fold ministry gifts carry the responsibility for the leadership of the Church here in the earth. They also have the God-given authority to fulfill those responsibilities. These responsibilities have not been given to the congregations, boards or committees. The Church is not a democracy. It is a theocracy. Jesus is the head of the Church, seated at the right hand of the Father where He reigns until He comes for us. Until that day we are commanded to occupy until He comes. Unfortunately, many Christians are in survival mode, not occupation mode. The reason is that the Church is not operating out of God's plan for occupation, but rather on man's plan of tradition.

God has set the members, every one of them, into the Church as it has pleased Him. Among the members are those called to the five-fold ministry as listed in Ephesians 4:11. It is essential that *every* believer first discover the measure of Christ, or the ministry gift of Christ, that he or she is, and then they must get into his or her place — the place in the Body where it has pleased the Lord to set them. According to Ephesians 4:11-16, there is no other way for the Church to become what the New Testament teaches it will be when Jesus returns for it. For this to happen, and it must happen, it will begin with the five-fold ministry gifts in place. These are the men and women whom God has anointed and equipped under the direction of the Head of the Church and by the power of the Holy Spirit. Ephesians 4:12 gives us the clear responsibilities of these gifts: the apostle, prophet, evangelist, pastor and teacher.

Ephesians 4:12

For the perfecting of the saints, for the work of the ministry, for the edifying of the of the body of Christ.

It has been the plan of God from the beginning for the work of the ministry to be accomplished by mature believers, equipped with ministry gifts and accompanied by the anointings. Unfortunately, that is far from what usually happens. The majority of believers perform their services for the kingdom of God within the local church by need, not by gift. Instead of discovering their ministry gifts and anointings, they end up either relying on natural talents and abilities or just doing their best to fulfill a need.

As a pastor, I am exceedingly thankful for all the courageous saints that were willing to put their hands to whatever needed to be done and then did it faithfully. Without those precious God-loving people, the church would not have produced the great fruit that it has. But their loving faithfulness still did not make it God's way. His way is what He describes in His Word. As fruitful as our church has been, how much more do you suppose we could have accomplished had we done things God's way?

Getting Into Place

I believe that we are in the beginning of a wonderful, fresh new move of God in the earth. It could very well be the move that ushers in the coming of the Lord Jesus for His Church. If that is true, the Church must become what the New Testament says it will be at His coming, and it must begin with the five-fold ministry.

Every great move of God in the past has not only produced great blessings for the world and for the Church but has actually restored certain powers and spiritual truths to the Church. I believe that this move will do the same. I believe that there will be great blessings in the form of multitudes being saved, baptized in the Holy Spirit, healed, delivered and set free. I also believe that there will be a great restoration of and in the Church. The restoration of the five-fold ministry gifts will be one of these blessings. When that happens, the Church will be put on a fast track to maturity that has not occurred since the days of its beginning.

Within the first forty years of its existence, the Church turned the world upside down, impacting the entire known world at that time. It happened under the supernatural power of the Holy Spirit working through the anointed ministry gifts.

The natural abilities and talents of mankind are magnificent. God created man in His own image and after his own likeness. Yet Jesus said, "Without me you can do nothing." If we toss out the traditions of men and embrace the New Testament plan of God, and if we allow Jesus to build His Church through His Body, can we even imagine the result?

Every move of God in the past has had both a spiritual and a natural focus. I believe that this new move will have the same. The spiritual focus will be on the Spirit and the Word. The natural focus will be on the local church that is the building block of the spiritual church. The local church is the predominant place where the perfecting of the saints is accomplished. The local church is where the Lord sets the great majority of the members of His Body as it pleases Him. In order for the saints to be perfected for the work of the ministry, the five-fold ministry must first come into its own place. I believe that will take place in the local church in a large measure.

The local church is headed up by the pastor. As the pastor goes, so goes his church. There is no such thing as a successful, high-impact church without a successful, high-impact pastor. Nothing happens without leadership. The problem we run into is that most pastors are not fully operating in their ministry gifts any more than their members are. My purpose for writing this book is not to be critical. It is to share some insight into what God has shown me in my own struggles as a pastor in an effort to bring about beneficial change. I believe it will help all of us to get where we want to be, into the pin-point center of the will of God.

The Struggles of a Pastor

It may be helpful for you to understand where I am coming from. For years I was a frustrated pastor, not in all areas but in some. My biggest area of frustration was in trying to understand my calling. I know other ministers who constantly doubt their callings. I never doubted my call once I recognized what it was, but I have been confused in trying to understand it. Since God told me to return to Nashville, Tennessee and plant a new church there, I have never doubted that I am called to pastor. My frustration was not in that. The problem was that I just did not seem to fit the mold of a pastor and the pastor's ministry as I understood it should be. Eventually, I discovered that it was not "the fit" that was the problem, but rather it was my understanding of what the ministry of a pastor was supposed to be.

I had developed preconceived ideas of what a pastor was all about, so I tried to force myself into that mold in some areas rather than follow the Holy Spirit as accurately as I should have. My biggest frustration came as I realized I had little, or no, anointing to do what I observed other pastors doing beyond the pulpit. My main nemesis was pastoral care ministry. For a long time I chalked it up to personality. It disturbed me that I did not have the right personality to be a good pastor when it came to meeting the needs of the people. I am not a natural "people-person extrovert." I love people, but most of the time I am not demonstrative in expressing that love.

After pastoring the same church for over thirty years, my congregation has grown to know that my wife and I love them deeply and that we have laid our lives down for them. In the earlier years they did not know that, and I did little to convey it to them openly. Out of the pulpit I am a rather private person. I am not an introvert, but for the most part I am not socially outgoing. I learned that this trait can be misunderstood by a congregation and by the pastor himself. When a pastor is like that, not only does the congregation begin to feel the pastor just doesn't love them, but he begins to question himself. I placed the same expectations on myself that my people did, and I ended up in frustration along with my congregation in the areas of pastoral responsibilities.

Finally, out of this dilemma I prayed to God for answers. In the next several chapters I share some of the insights that the Lord gave me. My desire is that this information will set you as free as it did for me. If you are a layman, I believe that it will give you a better understanding of your pastor's call and giftings. If you are a pastor, I hope to give you a better understanding of yourself and your gift.

The Five-Fold Ministry Giftings of Pastors

As I have had the opportunity to share this material in pastors' conferences and other places, I have literally watched pastors weep openly as their frustrations began to fall away, and the realization and understanding of their true calling began to emerge. I believe that you also can learn that you are not a fish out of water after all.

The simple truth is that no two pastors are alike. They not only have different personalities, but they have different ministry gifts as well. Not all pastors of a local church have the *five-fold ministry gift* of the "pastor," but he will have one or more of the five-fold gifts.

There are at least five kinds of pastors heading up local churches. They are apostolic pastors, prophetic pastors, evangelistic pastors, pastoral pastors and teaching pastors. Each one is different with very different characteristics in his ministry. Depending on the gift that he is to the church will determine the kind of church that he has and the eventual nature of his congregation. The following chapters will address each of these gifted pastors, their characteristics, their positives and their negatives.

By no means do I claim that these insights are completely definitive. They are merely the extent of my present understanding. My spiritual father used to regularly say from the pulpit, "eat the hay and spit out the sticks." It is my intent that what is written in this book will be hay, but if you encounter a stick or two, spit 'em out and move on!

CHAPTER THREE

The Five-Fold Gifted Pastors

Every person that is called to pastor a church has an accompanying gift from the five-fold ministry gifts. He should build his church through and upon that gift as God pleases. Each gift is given for a specific purpose and each church is to be placed in a specific area. As each church operates through its driving gift, the work of the ministry will be performed according to the plan God gave to Paul in Ephesians 4:11-13.

And he gave, some apostles; and some, prophets; and some, evangelists; and some, pastors and teachers;

For the perfecting of the saints, for the work of the ministry, for the edifying of the body of Christ:

Till we all come in the unity of the faith, and of the knowledge of the Son of God, unto a perfect man, unto the measure of the stature of the fulness of Christ.

When we started Victory Fellowship Church in 1977, the only spirit-filled influence of any real impact in the city was a local Full Gospel Business Men's Fellowship chapter and one other charismatic church that no longer exists. In the late 70's, Nashville, Tennessee was a stout denominational city, spiritually conservative and very traditional. The music in those churches was sung from hymnals of old and cherished songs. The atmosphere in most of our churches was stiff and formal and the Word was usually brief traditional doctrine, particular to whatever denomination the church happened to be. This geographical area was the center of the so-called "Bible-Belt" just thirty years ago. If the truth be told, that also describes the church, with some exceptions, as it existed all over the world at that time.

Early in the 1950's a world-changing revival began in the Church that continued for over fifty years. While the secular world has progressively become more and more carnal, the church has become more and more spiritual. Even so, the Church is still a long way from what Paul describes in Ephesians 4:13,…in *the unity of the faith, and of the knowledge of the Son of God, unto a perfect man, unto the measure of the stature of the fulness of Christ.* But we have come a long way from where we were.

In the following chapters we will identify some of the DNA which makes up each gift that accompanies the call to pastor, and we will explain its purpose. The first gift is the one that is most familiar to me because of my ministry, and that is the gift of the apostolic pastor. I will admit that I have a better understanding of this gift than others because it is my gift. Even so, I have lived in the heat of ministry for over thirty years, and during that time, through the realm of experience and the presence of God, I have learned much as I have observed both my own ministry and those of other pastors.

Early on in my ministry, some people tried to label me a prophet because of the proficiency of the revelation and inspirational gifts that are active in both my ministry and my wife's ministry. The office of the Prophet never really witnessed to me. I did not know what I was. I just knew that I was to plant and pioneer a local church. I did not discover my true ministry gift until much later as the Lord revealed the insights regarding the five-fold ministry callings of pastors that I share with you in this book. Before we can understand each individual calling we must understand the biblical descriptions of the five-fold giftings of pastors.

In preface to the following descriptions of the attributes of the five-fold pastoral ministry gifts, I want to emphasize that you cannot put God in a box. You cannot put people in a box either. All of the ministry gifts reside in human beings. No ministry gift will manifest exactly the same way in any two people, just as no two people are exactly alike. These descriptions are characteristics of a ministry gift abiding in a human being, not the description of a spiritual robot.

CHAPTER FOUR

The Apostolic Pastor

The first five-fold ministry gift named in Ephesians 4:11 is that of the apostle. This gift is often misunderstood and misinterpreted. For instance, I once heard the pastor of a large mega-church in the Midwest say that if he had it to do over he would have pioneered his church somewhere in the Sun Belt. When he said that I remember thinking that perhaps he had a choice of where he was supposed to be. As I thought about it though, I knew for certain that I was not given a choice. God specifically sent me to Nashville to pastor a church. Since then, Linda and I have traveled all over the world to preach the Gospel, but Nashville is our *place*. He sent us to impact this city with the Gospel.

God has dispatched His sent ones all over America and around the world for His purposes. Until the era of the Charismatic Renewal of the Church, the only Spirit-filled believers in local churches were in Pentecostal churches. In some parts of the country Pentecostal churches had significant influence, but in much of the country and the world they did not. So-called main-line denominational churches carried the most influence. Just forty years ago there were no Spirit-filled, Holy Ghost-baptized believers in these main-line churches. Today, virtually every main-line denominational church in Nashville has a significant number of Spirit-filled believers worshipping there. Many of them were filled with the Holy Spirit in my church and in churches like mine. This has happened, not just in Nashville, but all over the world.

Within the Charismatic Renewal there were several other moves of God that were a part of it. One of the most influential of those moves was the Word of Faith Teaching Revival. That particular move of God has been my primary circle of influence for the past thirty years. However, I do not confine myself to just one circle of influence or group. No one camp has everything that we need. Each camp has things that can benefit other camps.

When the Word of Faith Teaching Revival began, few people had a clue about how to live by faith. Today, multitudes do. More of the Word of God has been revealed to the Church in the past forty years than since the Apostle Paul himself preached it. The Church is better educated today in the Word of God than at any time since the first forty years of the Church Age. How did this happen? It has primarily been through apostolic pastors that were sent to strategic places, planting churches and perfecting the saints. The local church, however, has not been the only source of teaching. People have also benefited from what we call "para-church ministries" as well. Nationally known ministries have had a huge influence upon the Body through crusades, television, campmeetings and other areas, but without question the local church has carried the greatest influence in the life of believers.

When I started VFC in 1977, there was only one other "Word of Faith" church in the State of Tennessee, and it had only been in existence for one year. The independent Spirit-filled church did not exist in most places. Today, Nashville has hundreds of them. The country has thousands upon thousands, and the world has millions of Spirit-filled churches. Where did they come from? God's sent ones led the way. Many of these church leaders may not be apostolic pastors, and probably are not, but you can be sure that one or more of the Lord's *sent ones* paved the way in that particular area for what we are seeing today.

Visionary

An apostolic pastor is a visionary. He is not a detail-oriented person. That does not mean that he is not interested in details. He is! It means that he is a "big-picture person" that carries the overall vision for his church, but needs others to help him fulfill the details necessary to implement his vision.

The vision for a local church comes from the Head of the Church, Jesus Christ, not from the mind of man. A vision is not some grandiose extravaganza to propel any given local church into the world spotlight. It is simply the plan of God for that church.

When Jesus proclaimed that He would build His Church, He already knew what He wanted to build and how He wanted to build it. He had a vision from the Father. We know that because He said, "I only do what I see my Father do." That plan or vision included the local church as the primary building block of the worldwide spiritual Church. Therefore, the Father already had a plan for every local church that He ordained from before the foundation of the world. That is an awesome thought! Long before I was born, God already knew what He wanted my church to become and what it was to contribute to the building of His Church. In the fullness of time, he called me, an ordinary guy, to become an apostolic church builder. He imparted into my heart a strong vision for what He wanted this church to be and what He wanted it to do. That vision has become my life's purpose.

I have been committed to God's church building plan for over thirty years now, and I am not even slowing down, let alone quitting. I have no plans to ever retire. I will continue until I finish my course and then I will go home to be with Him, or until He comes for all of us, whichever comes first! If Jesus tarries, I believe that God's vision for VFC is much bigger than what I can fulfill during my tenure as its founding pastor. When I have completed my race, He will pass His plan on to future generations of pastors who will carry on the work until His return.

Builder of a Team

One of the attributes of a visionary is that he does not want to get bogged down with details. He wants to impart, or cast the vision onto others and let them do the work of actually implementing it. If it was the responsibility of the apostolic pastor to carry out the hands-on aspects of vision implementation, it would never happen. He is not equipped to do it. A visionary is rarely a hands-on person. That is why God will give him a team that learns how to work with the man of

God according to each person's gifting. The pastor informs the team of what he wants done, and they do it. It is that simple. It is not easy, but it is simple. Implementing the assignment for the church becomes easier as a church team, both salaried and volunteer, begins to understand the senior pastor's gift and how to work with it.

An apostolic pastor needs an apostolic team. By that I mean that he needs a team of people who understand the characteristics of an apostolic pastor and know how to effectively work together using those characteristics. It takes time to build such a team. You must find the right people, and then allow them the time to learn how to become an apostolic church team member. With patience an apostolic pastor will eventually pastor an apostolic church. The church will take on his ministry gift.

A Foundation Layer

Part of the apostolic gift is to lay a foundation. We know that Paul identified himself as a foundation layer.

1 Corinthians 3:9-11

For we are labourers together with God: ye are God's husbandry, ye are God's building,

According to the grace of God which is given unto me, as a wise masterbuilder, I have laid the foundation, and another buildeth thereon. But let every man take heed how he buildeth thereupon.

For other foundation can no man lay than that is laid, which is Jesus Christ.

The apostolic pastor's church will be a church rooted and grounded in the Word of God to the extent of the pastor's revelation in the Word. Some people have the notion that the ministry of an apostle is highly mystical and super-spiritual. They have been taught to believe that the apostle stands head and shoulders above all other gifts, almost to the point of breathing the rarified air of Heaven itself. They are under the assumption that his preaching and teaching is so deep and complicated that only a few people are mature and learned enough to really understand it. That is super-spiritual nonsense! The actual ministry of an apostolic pastor is that of a master builder. His personal specialty is foundational. He wants to build a strong foundation in every believer—a foundation that cannot be shaken when the winds blow and the floods of life come.

In my own ministry, there are certain foundational truths that flow through and infiltrate everything that I preach and teach regardless of what the subject is. The person in charge of our media ministry is in the process of converting over thirty-one years of taped messages to digital format and then placing them on a CD. He recently told me over lunch that I had preached over four-thousand messages in the church. If you could listen to a handful of those CDs, regardless of their subjects, you would hear how to develop a personal, intimate relationship with Jesus Christ; who you are in Him; what you have in Him; and what you can do in Him. You would also hear how to live by faith; how to walk in love; how to walk in the Spirit; how to have a solid, intimate prayer life; and how to live in the Spirit at all times. You would hear basic, foundational teaching.

In 1 Corinthians 2:1-5, the Apostle Paul describes the apostolic ministry both humbly and factually.

1 Corinthians 2:1-5

And I, brethren, when I came to you, came not with excellency of speech or of wisdom, declaring unto you the testimony of God.

For I determined not to know any thing among you, save Jesus Christ, and him crucified.

And I was with you in weakness, and in fear, and in much trembling.

And my speech and my preaching was not with enticing words of man's wisdom, but in demonstration of the Spirit and of power:

That your faith should not stand in the wisdom of men, but in the power of God.

Discoverer & Pioneer

There are basically three types of people in the world. They are discoverers, pioneers and settlers. All three are essential for the fulfillment of God's commandment to the human race as we read in Genesis 1:28, and to the Church in Matthew 28:18-20.

Genesis 1:28

And God blessed them, and God said unto them, Be fruitful, and multiply, and replenish the earth, and subdue it: and have dominion over the fish of the sea, and over the fowl of the air, and over every living thing that moveth upon the earth.

Matthew 28:18-20

And Jesus came and spake unto them, saying, All power is given unto me in heaven and in earth.

Go ye therefore, and teach all nations, baptizing them in the name of the Father, and of the Son, and of the Holy Ghost:

Teaching them to observe all things whatsoever I have commanded you: and lo, I am with you always, even unto the end of the world.

Discoverers are a rare breed indeed. They go where no one has gone before. Columbus was a discoverer as were Lewis and Clark. Geographically, there is no more of this earth left to discover, so those kinds of discoverers have shifted their attention to outer space. Others have taken their giftings to technology, medical research and other scientific and technical fields. There are spiritual discoverers as well. Martin Luther was one example, and John Wesley was another.

Every move of God that has occurred since the day of Pentecost has been initiated by a discoverer. Discoverers are innovators. They not only go where no one has gone before, but on the way they find new ways of doing things. Many of these new ways are rejected at first, but then eventually become a part of the fabric of our lives, making us stronger and better.

The leaders of the Pentecostal move were the spiritual discoverers during the first half of the twentieth century. They were the innovators. Men and women such as William Seymour, Howard Carter, P. C. Nelson, Lillian B. Yeoman, F. F. Bosworth and Smith Wigglesworth were a few of those. Most of these people were rejected in their ministries as extremists, but today they are regarded as heroes of faith.

The last half of the twentieth century saw men like Oral Roberts, Billy Graham, Kenneth E. Hagin and others lead the way in discovery and innovation. In no way do we want to exclude the vast numbers of faithful men and women known only to God and their immediate circle of influence. Their willingness to venture out of their comfort zones and into the unknown has paved the way for those of us in the earth today.

Following in the footsteps of the discoverer comes the pioneer. The pioneer is among the first ones to embrace the innovations of the discoverer. He recognizes the validity of the discoveries, embraces them for himself and boldly proclaims their virtues to others. There was a flood of pioneers who followed in Lewis and Clark's tracks from St. Louis to the Pacific. These men and women fought Indians, hardship, hunger, thirst, disease, weather, the plains, the mountains and sometimes one another, but they prevailed. Because of them we have a nation today that is blessed above all others.

There is a spiritual parallel in the Church. We have seen a flood of pioneers follow the discoverers in the Church over the past five-hundred years. They have embraced the discoveries and innovations of the discoverers and not only have they applied them to their own lives, but they have boldly proclaimed their virtues to all who had ears to hear. I was one of those pioneers and you may have been also.

Once the pioneer has gone forth, then comes the settler. The discoverer first goes where no one has gone before. The pioneer follows in his footsteps braving the hardships, taking the arrows and taming the land. The settler is equally a hero. He is the one who establishes the land by occupation. Jesus said, *"Occupy till I come."* (Luke 19:13). The settler battles the ordinary and the routine of everyday life to maintain his victory which is to establish his covenant and to keep the faith. All three types of people are necessary to the building of the Church.

The apostolic pastor and his flock will have an apostolic church. He will be a discoverer, or a pioneer, or both. For the first twenty years of my ministry I was a pioneer. After that I became both a pioneer and a discoverer. As difficult as pioneering is, the role of a discoverer is more so. Nevertheless, God's grace is more than sufficient. He has given us his Word in 1 John 5:4 saying *"...whatsoever is born of God overcometh the world: and this is the victory that overcometh the world, even our faith.*

A Builder

Paul called himself a wise masterbuilder. What was he referring to? He was a builder of what? He was speaking of the Church. Jesus said in Matthew 16:18, *"...I will build my church."* Jesus knew that shortly he was returning to the Father. He had no intention of building the Church through His own personal ministry which was about to come to its earthly end. He was aware that he was about to become the Head of the Church and would give gifts unto men for the building of the Church.

Ephesians 4:8

Wherefore he saith, When he ascended up on high, he led captivity captive, and gave gifts unto men.

Jesus' intention was and is to build His Church through the ministry gifts that He has set into the Body as it has pleased Him to do. All ministry gifts are builders, and apostles are masterbuilders. They are the ones that are sent to specific places with the building plans. Paul and the members of his apostolic team planted many of the churches mentioned in the New Testament. A major part of his ministry was planting churches.

Unlike most apostolic pastors today, Paul was never called to just one primary church. He was an apostolic traveling missionary, not an apostolic pastor. When he had established a local church to the point that he could install local leadership, he did so and then moved on to the next assignment. Even so, he never stopped offering each church his spiritual leadership and oversight. Why? Because he was a wise masterbuilder. He continued to build those churches through his visits, letters and team member visits. Apostolic pastors will do the same thing. They are rarely called to build just one church. Most will build the church that they are called to pastor themselves and plant other churches as well.

We have planted a number of churches out of VFC over the years, both in the United States and in Europe. Church planting is in the DNA of an apostolic pastor. He is in the church building business, both spiritually and naturally. Throughout my years of pastoring, I have never ceased building. We are constantly improving our facility in one way or another. It is in my DNA.

I also receive great joy when I help other ministers build their ministries. But my greatest joy comes from building people.

A Developer of People and Leaders

Our greatest example of apostolic people development is the ministry of Jesus, Himself. He is the greatest of all people-developers. We tend to place the most emphasis on His public ministry of preaching and teaching and His ministry to the multitudes. He healed the sick, raised the dead, cast out demons, worked miracles and walked on water. Sometimes we overlook the fact that He also developed the first leaders of the Church. This was a phenomenal feat. Jesus began with very raw material and had only three years to get a job done that would last for eternity. Most people could not have done in three lifetimes that which Jesus did in three years with His disciples. The fact is that once they were developed and fully equipped, they turned the world upside down and expanded the Church from Jerusalem to the entire known world in just forty years. And they did it in one generation!

People-development requires more than just knowledge. It requires an anointing. Not all ministry gifts have that anointing, but it is a part of the equipping of the apostolic pastor. I did not understand this until people in my church began to become strong leaders and ministers. Dozens of people were raised up into full-time ministry. I did not set out with a goal to develop and raise them up. It was not a planned ministry of the church. It just began to happen during the normal course of events in pastoring my church. It was the anointing that accompanied my ministry gift of apostolic pastor. I did not figure out these things by myself but discovered them in the process of years of ministry as God revealed them to me.

In the early nineties, our church had over fifty graduates from just one two-year international Bible college in the church. That was in addition to our two-year Bible school. During the nineties we had students from over one-hundred churches in the Nashville area coming to the Bible school in addition to the students from our own church. Several churches purchased special vans to transport their people to the school. These church leaders knew that we would not steal their sheep, but instead would develop, train, equip them and send them back to their churches to be a blessing there.

We have seen great fruit come from the ministries of this apostolic church. Today, there are full-time ministers that pastor their own churches. There are traveling ministers, missionaries on the foreign field, ministers on staff in other churches and on the staff in our own church. I have purposely never tried to count them up, and I will not. I will give the devil no place. Only God gets the glory.

None of this fruit was planned, and no knowledgeable attempt was made to produce it. The Apostle Paul describes the means, the motivation and the results of our actions in 1 Corinthians 15:10 and Ephesians 4:7.

1 Corinthians 15:10

But by the grace of God I am what I am: and his grace which was bestowed upon me was not in vain; but I laboured more abundantly than they all: yet not I, but the grace of God which was with me.

Ephesians 4:7

But unto every one of us is given grace according to the measure of the gift of Christ.

No flesh can boast. Without Jesus we can do nothing, but we are not without Him. He lives and ministers within us according to the measure of the gift of Christ that we are through grace.

God-Dependent, Not Man-Dependent

An apostolic pastor is self-reliant in his relationship with God and in his calling. He does not need, nor does he seek, the constant affirmation and approval of others. That does not mean that he becomes an arrogant lone ranger. It does mean that he is not emotionally needy. He is secure in his relationship with God and with his spouse, and that is enough for him.

God's vision for this pastor's church and ministry is clear in his heart and mind. He knows what God has called him to do, and he does it. Misunderstandings and criticism that may occur do not move an innovative discoverer. From the emotional standpoint, it really does not matter what other people think.

There are many people who need affirmation and approval, and this need can sometimes determine how effectively they fulfill the vision that God has given to them. We all need each other. No man is an island unto himself. We all need our families and friends, and we need associates in ministry to help us fulfill our calling. A wise pastor needs wise counsel in his ministry regardless of the ministry gift that he is. The apostolic pastor is as much in need of that counsel as anyone, but he has no need for the emotional support of others before he will make decisions. He is pleased when the affirmation and approval come, but he is not moved if it does not come.

Because this pastor is God-dependant and not man-dependant, he is not devastated when people fail him as sometimes they will. He may be disappointed, but not devastated. I have known pastors and people in general who are constantly frustrated, and many times devastated, by the failures of others, especially when those failures involve personal attacks or deceptions. Unfortunately, these things often happen in the ministry.

I have had people working in the ministry with me in whom I placed great confidence, but they failed to live up to that confidence. It is always disappointing but never overwhelming because my dependence is in God and not people. It is also true that I have a greater confidence in the God that is inside the people than I do in the people themselves. Living by this kind of faith is a characteristic required for the apostolic pastor's ministry who develops believers and raises up ministers. It is also a lesson learned from observing Jesus Himself.

When we consider the men that Jesus chose to become the Apostles of the Lamb and the founding leaders of the New Testament Church, and when we see their qualifications and backgrounds, we realize that Jesus definitely relied more upon God and the Holy Spirit within them than he did in the men themselves. When they failed him, and they often did, He did not panic and give up on them. Why? It was because He was God-dependent and not man-dependent. In the end all but one ran their races and finished strong.

A Risk-Taker

An apostolic pastor is a risk-taker. There is a difference between a reckless gambler and a risk-taker. There is rarely any great accomplishment without a risk. Many people never achieve great accomplishments because they are not risk-takers. They had rather settle for what they have than risk losing it in order to gain something greater.

In the natural, the closest description of an apostolic pastor is an entrepreneur. Webster defines entrepreneur as one who organizes and manages an enterprise, especially a business, usually with considerable initiative and risk. That definition also fits the apostolic pastor. Most apostolic pastors are also founding pastors. Founding and pioneering a church requires great initiative and considerable risk. Many of the characteristics of the apostolic pastor can also be found in business entrepreneurs. The only difference between the two is that one has a natural gift and the other is a spiritual ministry gift endowed with an anointing to fulfill that gift and to preach and teach the Gospel. We could easily say that an apostolic pastor is a spiritual entrepreneur. He is rarely satisfied with the status quo, always reaching for the next growth level. He will risk losing everything that he has accomplished to gain the next level. The apostolic pastor is not a reckless gambler going off on irresponsible tangents, fueled by fleshly ambitions. He is determined to fulfill the vision that God has given him. He is willing to pay whatever price it requires and to take whatever risk is necessary to reach the goal.

A Flagship Church

The ministry gift of the pastor will determine the nature of his church. An apostolic pastor will be a leader of leaders, a pastor of pastors. That is part of his gift. He is anointed to speak into the lives of leaders, especially pastors. Because of that, his church will be a leadership church.

We have a significant number of independent churches that are associated with our church. The Lord instructed me to name this association of churches and ministers Armada International. An armada is defined as a fleet of warships. One of the analogies of the Church and its mission in the earth is spiritual warfare. Individual believers are compared to soldiers. Each armada has a flagship which is usually the commander's ship and that commander is usually the admiral.

For the sake of clarity, all five-fold ministry gifts can be compared to military officers. I once heard a teacher say that the Bible compares believers to sheep because they are too dumb to think for themselves. I thought that statement to be a fine example of his questionable intelligence. Any analogy can be taken too far and arrive at wrong characteristics such as comparing believers to sheep. The analogies used to describe believers, such as soldiers, sheep, etc., are only to make a point.

All five-fold ministry gifts can be compared to military officers, but they do not all hold the same rank. Some are generals and admirals; others are colonels, majors and captains. Some are lieutenants starting out in their ministries. Each can progress in rank as he and his ministry matures, keeping in mind that promotion comes from the Lord and not from man. No one starts out in the place where he ends up. We all must grow and mature spiritually and ministerially.

As the apostolic pastor matures, he will usually become more and more influential both in his community and in his spiritual circle of influence. His church will become a flagship church in the city and often well beyond.

Misunderstandings and Misconceptions of an Apostolic Pastor

In summary, the apostolic pastor is a visionary. He is a big picture person who does not get involved with the intricate details of everyday vision fulfillment. He is usually a delegator of responsibilities and not a hands-on manager. As a result his staff can sometimes feel that he is too disengaged, and that they do not get enough personal attention and direction in the area of their responsibilities. Some may even feel that he does not care about their area of ministry, and that they are not appreciated or valued. This is almost always a misunderstanding. Unless something is deeply wrong on a personal level, pastors care very much about what is going on in their ministries, regardless of what ministry gift they may be. Apostolic pastors are just not detail people themselves. That does not mean that they do not care about details or that they do not want to be kept informed.

Staff members need to know what kind of pastor they are working with in order for them to be able to work with him more effectively. In the case of an apostolic pastor, the staff must learn to be more aggressive or pro-active with him and not depend on him to initiate their interactions. Most staff members need those interactions much more than he does. The apostolic pastor may not initiate those interactions as often or as much as some staff members need, but he is usually willing and eager to have the interactions because of his desire to form strong relationships which in turn will accomplish the goals for the mission.

Most apostolic pastors have a spirit of faith and confidence that can be intimidating to many people. They can appear to be unapproachable to some. The pastor, himself, is usually completely unaware of this persona. I have been told many times that I intimidate people just by showing up. That always surprises me when I hear it. Who me? I am just a big fuzzy-wuzzy love ball! How we feel, however, is not necessarily the way people perceive us. I have learned that I must be very purposeful in expressing loving kindness and warmth to people so that I will not intimidate them.

I have had folks come into my office for an appointment trembling with fear. Some of them have said, "I've wanted to come and talk to you for a long time, but I was too nervous or afraid to come!" I heard this so many times that I considered putting a sign on my door that said, "Principal's Office." I have learned to overcome these perceptions by overt actions of friendliness, kindness and people-person approachability even though that has not been my personality. The real truth is that once I formed the habit of conducting myself in that manner with people, I found that I really enjoyed it!

In summary, an apostolic pastor is God-dependent and not man-dependent. He is self-reliant in God, not needing the constant affirmation and approval of others. A person can misunderstand that characteristic thinking that the pastor does not like people. He may feel that the pastor is arrogant and too high and mighty for the common folk. Again, that is almost never true. Because the pastor does not emotionally need the approval of others is not an indication that he does not want it. Because he is not people-needy does not mean that he does not value and desire meaningful relationships. Because these perceptions can exist, it is the apostolic pastor's responsibility to overcome them by pursuing relationships from a Godly desire.

General Characteristics of an Apostolic Pastor

1. He is a sent one.
2. He is a visionary.
3. He is a foundation layer.
4. He is a discoverer or a pioneer, or both.
5. He is a builder.
6. He is a developer of people, especially leaders.
7. He is God-dependant, not man-dependant.
8. He is a risk-taker.
9. His church will be a flagship church.

CHAPTER FIVE

The Prophetic Pastor

Under the Old Covenant there were no born-again, Spirit-filled believers as we see them in the New Testament Church. During the time of the Old Covenant, the Holy Spirit only came upon God's appointed prophets, priests and kings. When Jesus was resurrected from the dead, we moved into His New Covenant ministry and received the Holy Spirit as prophesied in the Old Testament and fulfilled in the New Testament.

Psalm 68:18

Thou hast ascended on high, thou hast led captivity captive: thou hast received gifts for men; yea, for the rebellious also, that the LORD God might dwell among them.

Ephesians 4:8-11

Wherefore he saith, When he ascended up on high, he led captivity captive, and gave gifts unto men. (Now that he ascended, what is it but that he also descended first into the lower parts of the earth? He that descended is the same also that ascended up far above all heavens, that he might fill all things.) And he gave some, apostles;

and some, prophets; and some, evangelists; and some,
pastors and teachers.

The only gift mentioned above that existed under the Old Covenant was that of the prophet's ministry. Under the New Covenant, the prophet's ministry changed. Some of the characteristics of the prophet's ministry in both covenants are the same, but the purpose of the office is different. If someone under the Old Covenant wanted to hear from God, he had to pay a visit to the prophet. The priests ministered to God *on behalf of the people,* and the prophets spoke to the people *on behalf of God.* Under the New Covenant, God came to dwell with and in His people by the Holy Spirit, as prophesied by Jesus in John 14:15-17.

John 14:15-17

If ye love me, keep my commandments.

And I will pray the Father, and he shall give you another Comforter, that he may abide with you forever;

Even the Spirit of truth; whom the world cannot receive, because it seeth him not, neither knoweth him: but ye know him; for he dwelleth with you, and shall be in you.

Every believer can go directly to God for himself today. We do not need the prophet's ministry for guidance, but we still need the prophet's ministry. The prophet still speaks on behalf of God. He is an anointed preacher and foreteller of what God is doing in the earth at any given time.

A Cutting Edge Ministry

The prophetic pastor knows what God is saying and what God is doing. Reverend Lester Sumrall was a prophetic pastor. He used to say, "I have been in the forefront of every move of God in my lifetime," and he was! When you sit under the ministry of a true prophet, it seems that you are in the very presence of God Himself. That perception comes from the power of the prophet's anointing and his ministry purpose. He has been in the presence of God and he speaks forth what God is saying to His people. A powerful and intimate prayer life accompanies the prophet's ministry. He carries a boldness that no other ministry gift can quite match.

Direct and to the Point

The directness and boldness of the prophetic pastor will develop a tough, committed congregation. For those people who are called to him, this pastor will change their lives and give them hides like a walrus. It will not be long before these people have forgotten what it is like to get their feelings hurt. Pastors are generally known as being diplomatic. They have learned how to bring consensus among diverse agendas and opinions. Many pastors pride themselves in being able to calm troubled waters and make every person feel that his side prevailed in a given endeavor. Not so with a prophetic pastor. Talk about breaking the mold! This pastor does not give place to anyone's flesh or opinion that he feels is contrary to God's Word. He cares nothing for diplomacy. He only cares about what God wants to happen. He will speak boldly against sin, against worldliness and against the devil. His philosophy is, "Let the chips fall where they may!"

Brings Correction and Direction to the Body

A prophetic pastor will bring both correction and direction to the Body according to the extent of his influence and anointing. He cares nothing for political correctness. He will say whatever he believes God wants said regardless of who is present or what anyone thinks about it. Truth is his passion, integrity is his heart and purity is his motive. There is no room for compromise in him.

Pastors a Supernatural Church of Spiritual Gifts

This pastor will have a prophetic, cutting-edge church. Because congregations follow their pastor's lead, they will be fluent in the operations and manifestations of the Holy Spirit and will become fluent in the gifts of the Spirit over a period of time. The emphasis of a prophetic pastor's ministry will be on revelation gifts and prophecy.

The prophetic pastor's church will not have the typical Charismatic or Pentecostal congregation where people are content to observe the Holy Spirit move through others. This congregation desires to be used by the Holy Spirit themselves and will become operative in the moving of the Spirit in their services.

Misunderstandings and Misconceptions of a Prophetic Pastor

The prophetic pastor's church will be a supernatural church with a prophetic spirit about it. It may seem flaky to some that are not familiar with a prophetic church. Many of the operations of the Holy Spirit, especially those through the prophetic ministry gifts, may be dramatic and even flamboyant.

This pastor's boldness and demeanor can be mistaken for arrogant insensitivity to the feelings of others. In actuality he does not wish to offend people any more than other pastors. However, because of his giftings and anointings, he carries a boldness that may be hard for some people to handle.

The prophetic church may not only experience a larger expression of the manifestations of the Holy Spirit than some other churches, but it may also experience a larger expression of the human flesh as well. There is no such thing as spiritual fire without some wildfire along with it. If a church is not willing to deal with some fleshy demonstrations, it will not have the real demonstrations either. People learn to flow in the Spirit accurately through practice. If they are not comfortable to step out and learn through their own experiences, they will pull back. If a person sees someone publicly called down and embarrassed in his attempt to obey the Holy Spirit and who missed in the effort, then that person will never try to step out for himself. Having a truly supernatural church with good church order takes a very wise church leadership who is willing to walk a very thin line. For the prophetic pastor, this kind of leadership is essential.

Another danger for the prophetic pastor happens when everyone in the congregation believes that he is a prophet also. They assume that because their pastor is prophetic and because they attend a prophetic church, they are also called to the prophetic office. If the church is large, a few (with emphasis on few) may be called to the office of prophet, but most are not. You can know that this misconception is prevalent when you observe small groups or individuals prophesying to one another all over the church and in the parking lots after a service. The prophetic pastor must be cautious and wise in handling these situations in order to protect his flock on the one hand and to preserve the move of the Holy Spirit on the other.

General Characteristics of the Prophetic Pastor

1. He will have a cutting-edge ministry.

2. He is direct and to the point, developing a tough, committed congregation.

3. He will bring correction and direction to the Body to the extent of his influence and anointing.

4. His church will be a supernatural church, active in the gifts of the Spirit, especially the revelation gifts and prophecy.

CHAPTER SIX

The Evangelistic Pastor

Most people's image of an evangelist is an enthusiastic, flashy preacher on a crusade platform. There are some evangelists that fit that image, but there are also many others that are very different with a variety of ministries that includes the evangelistic pastoral ministry. Regardless of the specific ministry gift a pastor may stand in, including the evangelistic gift, he must first and foremost have a pastor's heart. It is impossible to successfully pastor a church without a pastor's heart. If you wonder what defines a pastor's heart, it is God's own heart for His people that He supernaturally imparts to His pastors.

Many pastors today are founding pastors of their churches. When you begin to pastor a church you are a pastor to no one. It can take up to five years to become a pastor to your congregation. Until that time you are just their preacher. When I was just the preacher in those early years, I remember crying out to God, "Lord, give me the hearts of the people. I do not have their hearts." After I had prayed this way for some time, the Lord answered me, "I will...after you give them your heart!" I was stunned. I had not realized until then that I had not given my heart to the people. I was not dedicating myself to them as Jesus taught us in John 15:13.

John 15:13

Greater love hath no man than this, that a man lay down his life for his friends.

I repented to God, and right then and there gave my heart to the people He had given me to pastor. When I did that something powerful and supernatural happened. God gave me His heart for His people. I was given a pastor's heart. From that time on I saw my congregation, both individually and corporately, in a whole new way. I saw them as the people of God. I had a love for them that I had never known before. It was not long before the congregation began to realize that there had been a change in me. I did not tell them. I did not need to. I was allowing Jesus to love His people through me. As I did that I began to have the hearts of the people, and I have had them ever since.

What does that have to do with the evangelistic pastor? Only this—every pastor must have a pastor's heart for God. The evangelistic pastor will also have God's heart and passion for the lost.

God's Heart and Passion for the Lost

The evangelistic pastor will love people. He will love the saints that are in his church, and he will have a passion for the lost. He knows that most of the lost people are just "good" people without Jesus. He is also aware that some are rank sinners and others are even evil. Jesus did not distinguish between the degrees of "goodness" when He went to the cross. This pastor is very aware that Jesus loves sinners and died for every one of them, and he will transmit the love of Jesus for sinners to his church. A truly evangelistic church is awesome to behold.

Romans 5:8

But God commendeth his love toward us, in that, while we were yet sinners, Christ died for us.

I have learned many things from some evangelistic pastors in the past ten years. It has changed my attitude toward unbelievers and the role of the Church where they are concerned. For the first twenty years of my pastoral ministry, I was confined to a believer's culture. I directed my ministry to and designed my church for those that were already saved. As a result we reached many believers. Most of our increase came from "transfer growth." We had much less outreach to unbelievers. VFC was a *believer's culture* as the majority of today's churches are.

When unbelievers came into our church we did not allow them to do anything in the church but sit and listen to the Word until they were saved. After they were saved, we still did not allow them to do anything in the church for six months to a year until they "grew in the Word." We had a believer's mentality, not an outreach mentality.

In 1997, we celebrated our 20th church anniversary. VFC had been a church in revival for its entire twenty-year span. It was the revival known as the "Word of Faith Teaching Revival." Great numbers of people were saved during that teaching revival, but the focus was mostly geared toward believers.

The Lord told me in the year of our anniversary that our church was not prepared for the next move of God that was coming. He instructed me to get prepared and told me how to do it. By the end of the nineties and the turn of the new century and new millennium, the teaching revival as a move of God was over. Because of God's instructions, I was already preparing for the next move regardless of what it would be. I started by moving our church from a believer's only culture to become more of an outreach body for unbelievers. It is not easy to make that transition. As a matter of fact, it has been one of the most challenging and difficult things that I have ever done. It is not easy to change an entrenched culture anywhere, but it is especially difficult in a church. During that process I leaned on and learned much from evangelistic pastors.

One of the first things that I had to do was to change my attitude toward unbelievers working in the church. Now, when any person comes to our church, believer or unbeliever, the first thing we attempt to do is to give him something to do in the church. Obviously, there are many responsibilities in the church that an unbeliever is not equipped to do, but I learned that there are also many things that he can carry out.

A few years ago, we decided to upgrade our worship team to professional musicians. After all, Nashville is Music City, USA! If that kind of upgrade had happened during the first twenty years of the church, I would have instructed my worship pastor to find born-again, Spirit-filled musicians only. I would not have even considered the idea of allowing an unbeliever on my platform. Instead, I allowed the worship leader to hire the best that he could find. Some that he hired were born again, Spirit-filled believers. Others were unbelievers and others were believers, but seriously backslidden. One of the newly-hired agnostic members had his own professional secular rock band.

This unlikely group of people is made up of awesome musicians, and the outcome of this faith venture is that each of the backsliders has repented and is in full fellowship with the Lord again. The unbelievers are all born-again with great testimonies. Each member believes that Victory Fellowship Church is the greatest church on earth, and that I am the greatest pastor on earth, second only to Jesus. Some of these guys would never have set foot in a church, much less helped lead a worship service. As a result I have some of the most anointed, as well as talented, musicians in world-famous Music City, USA. It occurred because I learned to change my attitude toward unbelievers from some great evangelistic pastors who love sinners as well as believers.

Anointed Preacher and Exhorter

The ministry gift of the evangelist is exercised through an anointing, not through a preaching style. Not all evangelists preach with arms flailing and saliva spewing everywhere. Instead his anointing will be inspirational and designed to move people into the will of God.

I was raised going to church. Because of the family businesses that my father was involved in, we moved more often than most people that I knew when I was growing up. Because of that we were not always in the same church. We were all Southern Baptist. Most kids in our churches were saved as children in Sunday School, but because we moved around so much I was able to avoid the sharp eye of the Sunday School teacher for a long time.

I spent my final years of high school in the small town of Cotton Plant, Arkansas. My family owned a grocery store named West End Grocery. It was located on the western end of town at a three-point intersection. The store was on the southwest corner of the street and the First Baptist Church was across the street on the southeast corner. It was there that I got saved.

My family and I had been going to that church for some time. We had a good pastor, and he was an adequate preacher. Every Sunday we had a salvation message of some sort, and as a teenager I knew I needed to get saved. As Southern Baptists we all knew pretty much everything there was to know about salvation, or at least we thought we did, even if we were not saved ourselves. I knew that I was not saved and fought it every Sunday. At the end of his sermon the pastor gave "The Invitation," and we would sing the same song every Sunday, "Just As I Am." I knew the routine very well. We would sing the first, second and last verses and then I immediately got out of there.

I was under strong conviction from the Holy Spirit to get saved every Sunday, but I stubbornly did not want to give up the "old man!" Another reason I was so stubborn was that almost all of my friends were already saved, and I did not want them to know that I was not. Sunday after Sunday I stood there gripping the pew in front of me so tightly that my knuckles turned white. I battled the conviction of the Holy Spirit until it was a wonder that the wood that I was holding onto did not crack.

When I was sixteen, we had our fall revival, and a young evangelist named Homer Martinez came to preach. No preacher had ever made an impression on me as he did. He preached under a powerful evangelistic anointing. That anointing not only brought me under conviction, but it moved me beyond the knowledge of my need for salvation to a desire for it. His preaching made me want to get saved. I found myself down at the altar giving my life to Jesus Christ. That evangelistic anointing moved me to yield to the will of God for my life and for me to be born again. At that time I knew nothing about anointings, but I sure knew the effect it had on my life.

A Growing Church with a Simple Mission

Most churches are being built on transfer growth. The Evangelistic Pastor will build his church on convert growth. The majority of churches today have a believer's culture as we had at VFC before we began to make the transition. Their ministries are directed mostly to believers, and that develops a believer's culture. The evangelistic pastor will have an evangelistic culture in his church. His heart for unbelievers will begin to imbibe into the church. He will teach his congregation how to win souls. They will not only learn how to, they will also do it. This pastor's heart will become the congregation's heart.

An evangelistic church can be called an outreach church. It is an extroverted church, not an introverted one. The greatest joy of that church comes from winning souls, both one-on-one and also at the altar. This pastor almost always makes an impact on his community by reaching people.

Divine Healings and Miracles

The evangelistic pastor will usually have a significant number of divine healings and miracles in his church. In the Book of Acts, the first example that we have of an evangelist is Philip. When the disciples were scattered abroad, the scriptures say that Philip went down to Samaria and preached the gospel there.

Acts 8:5-7

Then Philip went down to the city of Samaria, and preached Christ unto them.

And the people with one accord gave heed unto those things which Philip spake, hearing and seeing the miracles which he did.

For unclean spirits, crying with loud voice, came out of many that were possessed with them: and many taken with palsies, and that were lame, were healed.

When Phillip preached the gospel, people were saved. They were also healed and miracles happened, so much so that Simon the sorcerer got saved and followed Philip around witnessing the healings, deliverances and miracles. When Peter and John arrived from Jerusalem to see what was going on, Simon attempted to purchase the anointing. His foolishness was rebuked, but the incident reveals the power and impact of the evangelist's anointing.

Misunderstandings and Misconceptions of an Evangelistic Pastor

The evangelistic pastor's church may appear to be shallow because of a lack of emphasis on discipleship. This church can suffer from the same kind of tunnel vision that other churches may experience. For example, a strong teaching church may major on discipleship to the neglect of evangelism. The teaching church will produce strong Christians but may not impact their community by reaching unbelievers. The evangelistic church, on the other hand, may have a strong outreach ministry and win many souls, but it may not follow through with discipleship, resulting in immature Christians. The congregation can end up zealous for souls but remain spiritually shallow. Both of these issues are addressed in another chapter of this book.

The evangelistic church may appear to be carnal because of the abundance of sin in the camp. That can happen as a result of a high population of recent converts. It takes time for the sins of the flesh to fall away to holiness. The new birth is an event that changes our spiritual nature and makes us a new creation in Christ Jesus, but holiness is a process of spiritual growth. The truth is that there is plenty of sin to go around in all kinds of churches. The difference is that some older Christians have learned the fine art of covering up their sins, hiding them from one another, while the new convert does not even know that what he is doing is wrong. For that reason the evangelistic church may have less sin-conscience people than the more established Christians of other churches.

General Characteristics of the Evangelistic Pastor

1. The evangelistic pastor will not only have a pastor's heart for God's people, but he will also have a heart for the lost. He will have a heart for unbelievers as well as believers.

2. He will be an anointed preacher and exhorter.

3. He will usually have a growing church with a simple mission—reaching people.

4. He will usually have significant divine healings and miracles in his church.

CHAPTER SEVEN

The Pastoral Pastor

This minister is the model that most pastors and people acknowledge. The single-gift standard has resulted in much confusion, frustration and disappointment for everyone in the local-church world. The truth is that not every person who heads up a local church and is called "Pastor" will stand in the ministry gift of the pastoral pastor. For those who do, they can be a powerful blessing to the church. Those that do not stand in the pastoral gift must break out of the mold and build their churches on the gifts that they are. The anointing is upon the gift that each pastor is, and not on anyone's expectations. The purpose for this book is to make that distinction. The pastor that has received the pastoral gifting has a magnificent gift.

A Person of Love, Compassion and Strong Mercy

This pastor will be known for his love and compassion. 1 Corinthians 13 is the theme of his ministry.

1 Corinthians 13: 1-13

Though I speak with the tongues of men and of angels, and have not charity, I am become as sounding brass, or a tinkling cymbal.

And though I have the gift of prophecy, and understand all mysteries, and all knowledge; and though I have all faith, so that I could remove mountains, and have not charity, I am nothing.

And though I bestow all my goods to feed the poor, and though I give my body to be burned, and have not charity, it profiteth me nothing.

Charity suffereth long, and is kind; charity envieth not; charity vaunteth not itself, is not puffed up,

Doth not behave itself unseemingly, seeketh not her own, is not easily provoked, thinketh no evil;

Rejoiceth not in iniquity, but rejoiceth in the truth;

Beareth all things, believeth all things, hopeth all things, endureth all things.

Charity never faileth; but whether there be prophecies, they shall fail; whether there be tongues, they shall cease; whether there be knowledge, it shall vanish away.

For we know in part, and we prophesy in part.

But when that which is perfect is come, then that which is in part shall be done away.

When I was a child, I spake as a child, I understood as a child: I thought as a child: but when I became a man, I put away childish things.

For now we see through a glass, darkly; but then face to face: now I know in part; but then shall I know even as also I am known.

And now abideth faith, hope, charity, these three; but the greatest of these is charity.

The Greek word translated "charity" in the King James Version is "agape." Virtually all modern translations use the word "love." The Greek language of the New Testament is highly regarded for its expressiveness. It contains a number of words for the one word, "love." Each one describes a different kind or degree of love with the word, "agape," the highest. Some call it "the God-kind of love."

The ministry gift of a pastoral pastor is that he has a unique anointing to love people. All born-again believers have the love nature of God abiding in them, and all are commanded to walk in love; but the pastoral pastor has been given an anointing to love as a characteristic of his gift. This love in action is the giving of oneself for another. It is not just an emotion or a feeling. It is a power force in action. Jesus describes it this way in John 15:12-14.

John 15:12-14

This is my commandment, That ye love one another, as I have loved you.

Greater love hath no man than this, that a man lay down his life for his friends.

Ye are my friends, if ye do whatsoever I command you.

That kind of love is released into action by compassion. Jesus demonstrated that in Matthew 9:36. *But when he saw the multitudes, he was moved with compassion on them, because they fainted, and were scattered abroad, as sheep having no shepherd.*

Compassion is the recognition of and the identification with someone's need, accompanied by a deep desire to meet or alleviate that need. The pastoral pastor lives his life motivated by this love and compassion. It is a vital part of his gift. He does not have to work it up; it is just in his DNA.

The pastoral pastor will often have a strong mercy motive that will help him identify with each person's situation. Romans 12:6-8 identifies seven gifts that accompany ministry gifts for the purpose of motivation. These gifts are an imparted grace that empowers each ministry gift with the heart, or motivation, of God rather than that of the flesh.

Romans 12:6-8

Having then gifts differing according to the grace that is given to us, whether prophecy, let us prophesy according to the proportion of faith;

Or ministry, let us wait on our ministering; or he that teacheth, on teaching;

Or he that exhorteth, on exhortation: he that giveth, let him do it with simplicity; he that ruleth, with diligence; he that showeth mercy, with cheerfulness.

The pastoral pastor's strongest motivational gift is mercy. (If you have further interest in the motive gifts, I recommend the teaching of Dr. Marilyn Hickey on the subject.)

A Man Greatly Loved By His People

The law of seedtime and harvest is at work in the life and
ministry of a shepherd, especially if he is a long-term pastor.
When people have crisis situations in their lives and this
anointed pastor is there for them, helping them walk through
it in faith and the love of God, they never, ever forget it, nor
does Jesus.

Galatians 6:7-9

*Be not deceived; God is not mocked: for whatsoever a
man soweth, that shall he also reap.*

*For he that soweth to his flesh shall of the flesh reap
corruption; but he that soweth to the Spirit shall of the
Spirit reap life everlasting.*

*And let us not be weary in well doing: for in due season
we shall reap, if we faint not.*

Matthew 25:34-40

*Then shall the King say unto them on his right hand,
Come, ye blessed of my Father, inherit the kingdom
prepared for you from the foundation of the world:*

*For I was an hungered, and ye gave me meat: I was
thirsty, and ye gave me drink: I was a stranger, and ye
took me in:*

*Naked, and ye clothed me: I was sick, and ye visited me:
I was in prison, and ye came unto me.*

*Then shall the righteous answer him, saying, Lord,
when saw we thee an hungered, and fed thee? or thirsty,
and gave thee drink?*

When saw we thee a stranger, and took thee in? or naked, and clothed thee?

Or when saw we thee sick, or in prison, and came unto thee?

And the King shall answer and say unto them, Verily I say unto you, Inasmuch as ye have done it unto one of the least of these my brethren, ye have done it unto me.

Most Fulfilled When Immersed in Pastoral Care Ministry

For twenty years I had an associate pastor who was this guy. He retired from his position in 2000. He went home to Jesus and his reward seven years later at the age of 83. Jim Bledsoe was one of the greatest friends of my life, and I miss him greatly.

When this great pastoral pastor walked into a hospital room, the whole atmosphere changed. It was almost like Jesus had come through the door. Pastor Jim always knew exactly what to say and what to do. Any anointed man or woman of God can visit the sick and pray the prayer of faith, but when the anointed pastoral shepherd walks in, there is a significant difference.

This man of God did not have a strong pulpit ministry. There are many pastoral pastors that do, but not Jim. That was not his gift. His gift was to put the devil on the run. He helped raise people out of their need, whether it was sickness, financial, or family situations, and he put them on the road to victory in Jesus. He was greatly loved by the saints of VFC. During the final hours of his life, Pastor Jim paved his road to heaven with praise, waiting to hear, "Well done thy good and faithful servant!"

Personality of His Church

The pastoral pastor's church will be known for strong member relationships, deep fellowship, and friendliness to guests. It will provide splendid care for the flock. All of this will come forth out of this pastor's gift.

My family and I attended a fairly large church with a pastoral pastor like that for a period of time just before I began my own pastorate. At the time I had no idea why the church was like it was. The pastor was a good friend of mine and I knew that he was an extraordinary pastor, but I did not understand the distinctions of the pastoral ministry gifts. I just knew that I was not like him. When we established VFC, the atmosphere and culture were very different from my friend's church, reflecting who we were. Even so, I have never forgotten how wonderful it felt to walk into that church and literally be immersed in the atmosphere of a true shepherd's love.

Misunderstandings and Misconceptions of a Pastoral Pastor

One of the characteristics of the culture of a pastoral pastor's church is intimacy. The difficulty is that people can cherish the intimacy to the point of becoming an introverted church. If that is allowed to happen it will stunt the church's growth.

When VFC was very small I remember one lady saying to me, "I just love our little church. I hope that it never becomes so big that we lose what we have here." She was referring to our intimacy. She was not aware that intimacy is not the fruit of small churches. It is the fruit of love. If the people are taught that the various cultures of the pastoral gifts are a fruit of the anointings of those gifts and not a natural personality trait, they will not become introverted. They can preserve the culture of their church and still fulfill the Great Commission.

The pastoral pastor is motivated by a strong love and compassion for people. He must be on guard not to allow this motivation to interfere with some of the other duties of the senior pastor, such as discipline. A sound church must have good order, and good order requires discipline. I have known some wonderful pastoral pastors who refused to discipline anyone for anything, all in the name of love. They ended up with a church where every man is doing what seems right in his own eyes. That brings confusion to the flock and disorder to the services and other areas of the church. We are admonished by the Apostle Paul in Ephesians 4:15 to *speak the truth in love (that) we may grow up into him in all things, which is the head, even Christ.* No pastor should ever allow an "anything goes" attitude to form in his church.

General Characteristics of the Pastoral Pastor

1. He will be a man known for love and compassion.

2. He will often have a strong mercy motive that helps him to identify with every person's situation.

3. He will be greatly loved by his people.

4. He will be most fulfilled when he is immersed in pastoral care ministry.

5. His church will be known for strong member relationships, deep fellowship, friendliness to guests and its splendid care for the flock.

CHAPTER EIGHT

The Teaching Pastor

The teaching pastor is a fascinating gift. I have known some of the finest teachers in the Body of Christ. In the late nineties we saw the completion of a powerful and exceedingly fruitful thirty-year teaching revival that was a major part of the great Charismatic Renewal. This teaching revival not only affected the American Church, it impacted the world. The Body of Christ today consists of the most well taught Christians since the Apostle Paul taught the Pauline revelation of redemption during his lifetime. Even so, there are still multitudes of Christians who have not been well-taught in the Word of God. There are also multitudes who have been taught well, and these Christians are dramatically changing the Church and the world.

During the teaching revival, the teacher became the most prominent gift. Entire camps of teaching churches were birthed all over the world. That revival may have run its course as a move of God, but the need for teachers will never cease in the Body of Christ.

We must point out that there are differences in teaching gifts. Many people, both believers and unbelievers alike, have a natural talent for teaching. That is a needed ability in the Church and in the world, but it is not to be confused with the ministry gift of the teacher. The talent to teach carries natural abilities but does not carry the supernatural anointing to teach. The ministry gift of teacher does.

There are differences in the ministry gifts of the teacher. What we term "lay-persons," or those who are not called to the five-fold ministry, can have a ministry gift of teaching accompanied by the anointing to teach. That is not the same as the five-fold ministry gift of teacher as mentioned in Ephesians 4:11. All of the five-fold gifts can be apt to teach, including pastors, but being apt to teach is not the same as standing in the office of the teacher.

I love to teach, and it does not matter whether it is one-on-one, in a small group, before the whole church or in conventions of thousands. I have a teaching gift even though I do not stand in the office of the teacher. I stand in the offices of apostle and pastor. I am an apostolic pastor. The man that does stand in the office of the pastor and teacher will have the following characteristics.

A Man of Insight and Information

This pastor will receive supernatural insight into the scriptures. That can be said of all ministry gifts that are gifted to teach, but for the teaching pastor it will have an added dynamic. When you are sitting under the ministry of a teaching pastor, he may say something that will make you wonder, "Where did he get that?" Over the years I have sat under the ministries of many fine men and women who have a gift to teach, but the person who has the five-fold ministry gift of teacher is in a class by himself. He will bring out information that no other teacher can. That is his anointing. I could give you many examples of this gift, but I am quite sure that you are also familiar with many of these gifted men and women.

An Attention Holder

Some people are of the opinion that teachers are dry and boring. If someone thinks that way, it is only because he has never sat under a true teaching pastor. This pastor can hold the attention of the congregation longer than any other of the five-fold anointings. Multitudes learned that during the teaching revival era. They found that the teaching pastor is exciting and inspirational with an anointing to create a spiritual hunger in his listeners for the Word of God. People literally sat for hours with their spirits open like the mouths of baby birds in their nest. The ministry of the teacher has blessed my life and the lives of many in measures and ways that are inexpressible.

A Producer of Revelation Knowledge

The teaching pastor's anointing is designed to produce revelation knowledge in the hearts of believers. God spoke through the prophet Hosea in Chapter 4:6, *My people are destroyed for lack of knowledge.*

There is a difference between intellectual knowledge and revelation knowledge. The first is natural and the second is spiritual. The purpose of the Word of God is to reveal God and His will to man. This knowledge must be revealed. We are told in 1 Corinthians 2:14 that it cannot be discovered through natural means.

1 Corinthians 2:14

But the natural man receiveth not the things of the Spirit of God: for they are foolishness unto him: neither can he know them, because they are spiritually discerned.

This revealed knowledge is what we call revelation knowledge, and it is through that knowledge that we can live the abundant life that God desires for us to have. It is the life that Jesus was sent to earth to give to us.

John 10:10

The thief cometh not, but for to steal, and to kill, and to destroy: I am come that they might have life, and that they might have it more abundantly.

2 Peter 1:3, 4

According as his divine power hath given unto us all things that pertain unto life and godliness, through the knowledge of him that hath called us to glory and virtue:

Whereby are given unto us exceeding great and precious promises: that by these ye might be partakers of the divine nature, having escaped the corruption that is in the world through lust.

Many people have read and studied the Bible for a lifetime and have heard it preached as well, yet they have never achieved this manner of life. The reason is the difference between intellectual knowledge and revelation knowledge. A person can memorize the Bible from Genesis to Revelation and yet it will not become real to him. If it is not real to the person then he cannot live it, and the promises of God will be of no effect in his life. It is only through revelation knowledge that the Word of God and His promises become reality to us. That reality produces faith and we know that the just shall live by faith.

Romans 1:16, 17

For I am not ashamed of the gospel of Christ: for it is the power of God unto salvation to every one that believeth; to the Jew first, and also to the Greek.

For therein is the righteousness of God revealed from faith to faith: as it is written, The just shall live by faith.

Romans 10:17

So then faith cometh by hearing, and hearing by the word of God.

When we sit under the ministry of a true teaching pastor, revelation will come if our spirits are open. It comes by the anointing of the Holy Spirit that is upon the ministry gift of a teacher. There is nothing quite like the spiritual thrill that happens when sudden revelation unfolds. When that portion of God's Word comes alive to us it becomes real. Now we are able to live it, not in a religious way, but in the way of God. More of His abundant life becomes ours.

When I was baptized in the Holy Spirit in 1973, I greatly expanded my circle of influence in the Body of Christ. Until then I rarely ventured outside the boundaries of my denomination. I had no reason to. Once I was filled with the Holy Spirit, I became active in the Full Gospel Business Men's Fellowship International. Through that organization and other charismatic influences I began to hear many teachings on faith and the promises of God that I had never heard in my denominational experience. I listened intently to these and other teachings because I was spiritually hungry and wanted to learn all that I could. As I listened, revelation began to come, here a little and there a little, but the message of faith and the promises of God eluded me. I wanted to believe it, and I tried to believe it, but it just was not real to me. I was being taught intellectually, but there was no reality to it for me. It all seemed like a fairy tale. Intellectually, I knew that it was true because it was in the Bible, but it wasn't truth to me experientially. That can apply to many people. All truth is just a concept until we actually experience it. Then it becomes reality.

In the fall of 1975, I attended a Full Gospel Business Men's Fellowship International Regional Convention at a downtown hotel in Nashville. An up-and-coming young teaching pastor from California was the guest speaker for the afternoon teaching sessions. Two things struck me: I had never sat under the teaching of a young black man before, and I had never sat under the teaching of a true teaching pastor. I will forever be in that young preacher's debt. He taught on the subject, "How Faith Works," from Mark, Chapter 11. My life was changed forever in those three, one-hour afternoon teaching sessions. I got it! Finally, the lights came on! The revelation of what faith is and how faith works flooded my spirit and soul. I have never been the same since that conference, nor ever will be again.

When I left that convention I immediately began to practice what I had learned. I began to live by faith. My faith worked and has never stopped working. Why? It is because the Word of faith became reality to me. I received revelation knowledge. That is the marvel of the anointing on God's gifted teachers. It brings the Word of God alive to people. I have received revelation knowledge of many things in God's Word since then, but that experience stands out for me because it was the first revelation knowledge I received, and it was life-changing. It came through the ministry of the teaching pastor.

Studying the Word & Preparing Teachings

Most of those who have the preaching and teaching gifts find their greatest fulfillment in delivering their messages more than they do in studying and preparing for them. The five-fold teacher is just the opposite. He can study for hours on end and still go back for more. The teacher wants to understand every nuance of every word in the Bible on every subject. He will surround himself with multiple versions of the Bible, commentaries and books written by others on the subject he is studying. With today's computer technology it is much faster and easier to do that.

[As a side note I want to encourage every person, especially pastors and ministers, to embrace the wonderful tools available through computer technology. Thank God for the wonderful software that is available today. I resisted these tools for years simply because I did not want to make the effort to become computer literate beyond email and other basic uses. I still have a long way to go, but I have learned enough to realize it is worth the effort to learn much more.]

A Congregation of Well-Educated Learners

The teaching pastor will draw a congregation of people that are well-educated in the Word of God. His congregation will consist of hungry believers. They will come with their Bibles, their notebooks and their desire to learn as much about God and his Word as they possibly can. The great teaching revival of the latter part of the twentieth century was the perfect environment for the teaching pastor. It beautifully showcased his ministry. In the process, his gift was partly responsible for the Body of Christ becoming the most spiritually well-educated Christians since that first generation of believers that turned the world upside down. It is time to do it again!

Misunderstandings and Misconceptions of a Teaching Pastor

The teaching pastor's church can become so focused on teaching and learning that it begins to suffer from spiritual obesity. The congregation can become so self-absorbed that they develop a *feed me, feed me* attitude. They can turn into learners for learning's sake instead of boldly living out their great redemption.

Pastor Rick Warren of Saddleback Church in Southern California wrote a fine forty-day devotional entitled, *The Purpose Driven Life*. The first words of the first chapter are, "It's not about you!" That statement summarizes a trap that a teaching church can fall into. The church can become so internalized that it becomes all about them with no purpose other than themselves. The people may begin to think exclusively in terms of "Jesus died for me, and the promises of God are given for me to be able to live an abundant life!"

If the teaching pastor is faithful to preach the whole counsel of God, his congregation will discover that although this statement is true, it is not the whole truth. They will see that it is for them, but not for them exclusively. We know that Jesus died for all mankind, and that His gospel is for everyone. It is the responsibility of those who have been given the truth to take the good news to those who do not have it.

On the northern end of Israel, the Jordan River flows into the beautiful fresh water that the Bible calls the Sea of Galilee. It is deep and full of life. I have stood on its shores and have ridden on its waters several times. This lake has been giving life to that region of Israel for thousands of years. At the south end of the lake, the Jordan River flows out of the Sea of Galilee and continues its journey until it pours into another body of water that is called the Dead Sea. That is where the Jordan River stops. Unlike the Sea of Galilee, there is no life in The Dead Sea, even though it is being filled with the *alive* Jordan River. The same waters that flow into the Sea of Galilee flow into the Dead Sea. The difference is that the Dead Sea has no outlet. It is contained within itself and does not share its life. Therefore it dies. The area around the Sea of Galilee is beautiful. It is green and full of life. The area around the Dead Sea is a desert.

We must not let our churches become so focused on ourselves that our lives and our fruit become like the Dead Sea that cries, "Feed me! Feed me!" The Jordan River pours its life into it, but what does the Dead Sea do with that life-giving water? It consumes it on itself and dies. James 4:2, 3 says, *Ye lust, and have not: ye kill, and desire to have, and cannot obtain: ye fight and war, yet ye have not, because ye ask not. Ye ask, and receive not, because ye ask amiss, that ye may consume it upon your own lusts.*

General Characteristics of the Teaching Pastor

1. He is a man of insight and information.

2. His anointing can hold the attention of a congregation longer than any other of the five-fold anointings.

3. His anointing is designed to produce revelation knowledge in the hearts of believers.

4. His greatest fulfillment is in studying the Word of God.

5. His church will be a congregation of well-educated learners.

CHAPTER NINE

Building the Church

Matthew 16:18

And I say also unto thee…I will build my church; and the gates of hell shall not prevail against it.

For two thousand years, Jesus has been building His church. Ministry gifts and the local church are His primary building materials. The Church, or the entity being built, is not an institution, an organization, a business enterprise, a real estate venture or even a religion. Here on this earth, the Church has elements of all of these, but they are only to meet natural necessities. The Church is the called-out assembly of the people of God. When Jesus said, "I will build my church," He was talking about building people. That is also what Paul was speaking of in Ephesians 4:11-16.

Ephesians 4:11-16

And he gave some, apostles; and some, prophets; and some, evangelists; and some, pastors and teachers;

For the perfecting of the saints, for the work of the ministry, for the edifying of the body of Christ:

> *Till we all come in the unity of the faith, and of the knowledge of the Son of God, unto a perfect man, unto the measure of the stature of the fulness of Christ:*
>
> *That we henceforth be no more children, tossed to and fro, and carried about with every wind of doctrine, but the sleight of men, and cunning craftiness, whereby they lie in wait to deceive.*
>
> *But speaking the truth in love may grow up into him in all things, which is the head, even Christ:*
>
> *From whom the whole body fitly joined together and compacted by that which every joint supplieth, according to the effectual working in the measure of every part, maketh increase of the body unto the edifying of itself in love.*

The five-fold ministry gifts build the church by building people. The builders are not all pastors. Paul wasn't. But I believe that most of these gifts are either senior or staff pastors. Each of these pastors has great strengths. Those strengths will determine and produce the kind of mission emphasis each church will have. To have God's highest and best, each pastor must build his church on the gift of Christ that he is, and the anointings that accompany the gift. But, no matter how strong a pastor's gift is, his gift alone will never be enough to build a church. A truly great church requires the gifts and anointings of a committed leadership team and the entire congregation.

The senior pastor's gift and anointings will determine the mission emphasis of his church, but no single five-fold gift can fulfill all five scriptural purposes of the local church. I mentioned Rick Warren's best-selling book, *The Purpose Driven Life*, but before he wrote that book, he wrote *The Purpose Driven Church*. In the first book he identifies five scriptural purposes that every church should endeavor to fulfill. They are Worship, Evangelism, Fellowship, Discipleship and Ministry. No single pastoral gift can accomplish all these goals. That means that we must either have a church for each purpose, or we must have a church that accomplishes all five purposes. I believe that the latter is by far the most efficient. In order to do that, each pastoral gift must surround himself with the strengths and gifts that he does not have. That can be a monumental task, one that in the natural may never be accomplished, but the difficulty level is no reason for not trying.

The vast majority of churches are not in a financial position to have a paid staff of anointed ministers to accomplish the goals that are set before them. Even if they were, finding the right people who are the right fit, with the right anointings could take a lifetime. The first thing that a pastor must do is to forget about trying to do this by natural effort, and then begin to do it by faith. You cannot wait for the perfect people to show up. You must start with the ones you have. Remember that the Lord sets the members in the body as it pleases Him. God called you, gifted you and assigned you. He knows what you need and who you need to accomplish what He has called you to do. Do not just put willing vessels wherever a need exists. First, you must identify the gifts that are in your congregation and match the gift with a ministry that fits the anointing. Keep in mind that you are building your church, and that it is a lifetime project. You are not assembling a model that has all the pieces present. You are building your church by building people.

Over the years people will come and go. That means that in the local church you will never reach completion. You will always be starting over. The local church is a people entity. It ebbs and flows with gifts and anointings. It is never static. At any given time your church is only capable of producing the fruit of the ministry gifts you have available. Everything else is wasted effort. In order to produce the greatest fruit possible, you must constantly be identifying the gifts and anointings that you have, and match them with the ministries that go with their anointings. That is a whole new approach to local church ministry for most pastors, but it is the best.

Most churches are program-conscious which means they are need-driven. The pastor will identify a need and develop a program to operate a ministry to meet that need. He will then find someone to run the program. As a result, the number of people that are actively working in church ministry will be limited to the number of people required to operate its programs. This accounts for the statistics that show twenty percent of people in the church do eighty percent of the work, and also do eighty percent of the giving. There are always exceptions to these statistics, but it is true for many of our churches.

The local church is in need of some innovative ways of doing things. The old traditional ways that we have followed are not building the church according to the New Testament model. Jesus, the Head of the Church, is about to shake things up! Instead of churches being program-conscious and need-driven, they will be ministry-gift conscious and purpose-driven. In his book, Pastor Rick uses the baseball diamond to illustrate the five purposes of the local church. He puts worship on the pitcher's mound, evangelism at home plate, fellowship at first base, discipleship on second, and ministry on third base. Worship represents the corporate worship services of the church; evangelism is the outreach ministries; fellowship is the membership ministries; discipleship is the spiritual growth ministries; and ministry incorporates the various programs or ministries of the church apart from outreach.

The five purposes of a local church are those elements that I gleaned from Saddleback for my church. I had been pursuing those purposes for years but did not have an identity for them. After I returned from those conferences, I ran across notes from an old vision-casting sermon from several years before. I had preached those same five purposes to my church, but they were not nearly as well developed or organized into a usable concept. When we find a usable concept, we cannot automatically implement it as a program, find a warm body to head it up and expect the program to be successful. The anointed ministry gifts in our church will determine what we can put into operation. We must change our approach to be successful.

What does it mean to be ministry-gift conscious and purpose-driven? It means that you know the purposes of your local church. You have those purposes in place in vision form but you do not pursue the purposes. You pursue the gifts that you have in your church, identifying them and placing them into the ministries that match their gifts.

There are certain ministries that every church must have to function. It must have a pastor, and it must have people to be pastored. Beyond that, nothing is absolutely necessary. As the church grows, other ministries will be developed. They are not developed on the basis of tradition, desires or even need. They are developed on the basis of ministry gifts. As a pastor, you must find the ministry gifts that are in your church and build on them in the same way that you build on your own pastoral gift.

When we operated our Bible school in the early eighties, it was by the leading of the Holy Spirit. I had a person with a good teaching gift and we had hungry Christians that wanted to learn. I thought that was all we needed. Our church ministry calendar has always run from September through June, with July and August set aside for vacations and preparations for the new church year. Our school began in September with great anticipation. Things went well until the Christmas break. When we returned from the break, we found that many students had dropped out. The attrition continued until we just stopped the classes altogether. That phenomenon happened several years in a row.

The school started out of a desire and a need and not from a ministry gift with an anointing to lead and develop it. In the mid-eighties there was a young woman in our church who had graduated from a Bible school in another state. The Lord impressed upon me to offer her the Bible school ministry. I did, and she accepted. At that time I still did not have in-depth knowledge of ministry gifts, so the offer was not based on her gift. I was led by the Holy Spirit to make the offer. It turned out that her ministry gift was teaching, organizing and developing. What I had been unable to accomplish for several years, she was able to activate immediately. Two years later she married a young man in our church and they left for him to go to the same Bible school she had attended.

As it turned out, that lady's niece had just graduated from the same school and was returning to Nashville, and VFC. At the leading of the Holy Spirit, I offered the Bible school ministry to her. She had an even stronger anointing for the ministry than her aunt. This young woman ran the school for the next ten years. For a total of twelve years this Bible school was phenomenally successful under the ministries of these two women. Then, in the late nineties, this director also married a young man in our church and they soon left to pastor a church in a nearby city. After that we tried to keep the school going, but after a couple of years it was dead, so I buried it and moved on. In the next eight years I never ceased desiring a Bible school ministry, but I did not have a ministry gift available for it until recently.

In a few months my church prayer director is retiring from her nursing career. She is not only an anointed prayer warrior, but she is a teacher, a leader and a developer of people. She will develop and direct the new Abundant Life University that will contribute to our discipleship purpose.

I have learned the way to start church ministries. I have become ministry-gift conscious and purpose driven. Until the gift becomes available, the purpose must wait. If we prioritize the purpose ahead of the gift we will have nothing but frustration and failure, but if we prioritize the ministry gift, we will have success in the great majority of our ministries.

CHAPTER TEN

Building the Church on Your Gift

Each of the five-fold pastors carries great strength. The strength will determine and produce the kind of mission emphasis that the church will have. The bottom line is that in order for us to reach God's highest and best, each pastor must build his church on the measure of the gift of Christ that he is. He must uncover this gift and learn how to work within it.

We must all recognize that no single gift can do everything. The individual gifts are not anointed to serve all needs. They are anointed to do specific things. What we must do is surround ourselves with people, both in staff and congregational volunteers such as Helps Ministries or Children's Ministries, to serve the needs of the people in all aspects of the church. We must set into place those gifts and anointings that we, ourselves, do not have.

One of the most important things for every pastor to understand is that no matter how strong his gift may be, that gift alone will never be enough to build a church. A truly great church requires the gifts and anointings of the entire congregation. It requires a staff of anointed and gifted men and women.

Many pastors make the mistake of hiring people just like themselves. That is the last thing he should do. It does not mean that a pastor should not want someone on staff who has the same gift that he has, but if each staff member is a clone of the pastor, then everyone in the church is in trouble. Its accomplishments will be limited to the fruit that gift can produce. The majority of the staff should be made up of people who carry the gifts and anointings that the pastor does not have. As he begins to see the fruit of these anointed ministries, he must guard against the feeling of being threatened by them. Instead it should be a time for rejoicing!

Continually build up your staff. Celebrate them. When you do, the people will receive them. Congregations have been accustomed to depending upon the senior pastor for all the needs of the church. Retraining them into God's better way will require time, patience and love.

The biggest problem that a senior pastor will have is getting his congregation to accept the ministry of someone other than himself when they have a need. It is one of the greatest hurdles that he will have to overcome. It will require a process of time-consuming training on his gifting and on the giftings of the leadership of the church. The end result will give his people a much better way of receiving the personal ministry they need, bringing forth greater fruit. Once they grasp hold of it and once they understand how the anointings within the church work together for the good of all, they will embrace the entire ministry that God has given them in the church. Then the pastor can take the limits off of all that he desires to accomplish the glory of God.

Printed in the United States
147351LV00002B/1/P